SWIMMING

Steps to Success

SWIMMING

Steps to Success

David G. Thomas, MS
Professor Emeritus
State University of New York–Binghamton

Leisure Press
Champaign, Illinois

Library of Congress Cataloging-in-Publication Data
Thomas, David G., 1924-
    Swimming—steps to success/David G. Thomas.
      p. cm.—(Steps to success activity series)
    ISBN 0-88011-309-X
    1. Swimming. I. Title. II. Series.
GV837.T47 1989
797.2′1—dc19   87-31851
                                                    CIP

Developmental Editor: Judy Patterson Wright, PhD
Production Director: Ernie Noa
Copy Editor: Peter Nelson
Assistant Editors: Kathy Kane and Steve Otto
Proofreader: Laurie McGee
Typesetter: Yvonne Winsor
Text Design: Keith Blomberg
Text Layout: Denise Mueller
Cover Design: Jack Davis
Cover Photo: Bill Morrow
Illustrations By: Bonnie Hammer and Tim Offenstein
Printed By: Phillips Brothers Printers

ISBN: 0-88011-309-X

Printed in the United States of America

10 9 8 7 6 5 4 3 2

Leisure Press
A Division of Human Kinetics Publishers, Inc.
Box 5076, Champaign, IL 61820
1-800-342-5457
1-800-334-3665 (in Illinois)

Contents

Series Preface

The Steps to Success Activity Series is a breakthrough in skill instruction through the development of complete learning progressions—the *steps to success*. These *steps* help students quickly perform basic skills successfully and prepare them to acquire advanced skills readily. At each step, students are encouraged to learn at their own pace and to integrate their new skills into the total action of the activity, which motivates them to achieve.

The unique features of the Steps to Success Activity Series are the result of comprehensive development—through analyzing existing activity books, incorporating the latest research from the sport sciences and consulting with students, instructors, teacher educators, and administrators. This groundwork pointed up the need for three different types of books—for participants, instructors, and teacher educators—which we have created and together comprise the Steps to Success Activity Series.

The *participant book* for each activity is a self-paced, step-by-step guide; learners can use it as a primary resource for a beginning activity class or as a self-instructional guide. The unique features of each *step* in the participant book include

- sequential illustrations that clearly show proper technique for all basic skills,
- helpful suggestions for detecting and correcting errors,
- excellent drill progressions with accompanying *Success Goals* for measuring performance, and
- a complete checklist for each basic skill for a trained observer to rate the learner's technique.

A comprehensive *instructor guide* accompanies the participant's book for each activity, emphasizing how to individualize instruction. Each *step* of the instructor's guide promotes successful teaching and learning with

- teaching cues (*Keys to Success*) that emphasize fluidity, rhythm, and wholeness,

- criterion-referenced rating charts for evaluating a participant's initial skill level,
- suggestions for observing and correcting typical errors,
- tips for group management and safety,
- ideas for adapting every drill to increase or decrease the difficulty level,
- quantitative evaluations for all drills (*Success Goals*), and
- a complete test bank of written questions.

The series textbook, *Instructional Design for Teaching Physical Activities*, explains the *steps to success* model, which is the basis for the Steps to Success Activity Series. Teacher educators can use this text in their professional preparation classes to help future teachers and coaches learn how to design effective physical activity programs in school, recreation, or community teaching and coaching settings.

After identifying the need for participant, instructor, and teacher educator texts, we refined the *steps to success* instructional design model and developed prototypes for the participant and the instructor books. Once these prototypes were fine-tuned, we carefully selected authors for the activities who were not only thoroughly familiar with their sports but had years of experience in teaching them. Each author had to be known as a gifted instructor who understands the teaching of sport so thoroughly that he or she could readily apply the *steps to success* model.

Next, all of the participant and instructor manuscripts were carefully developed to meet the guidelines of the *steps to success* model. Then our production team, along with outstanding artists, created a highly visual, user-friendly series of books.

The result: The Steps to Success Activity Series is the premier sports instructional series available today. The participant books are the best available for helping you to become a master player, the instructor guides will help you to become a master teacher, and the teacher educator's text prepares you to design your own programs.

This series would not have been possible without the contributions of the following:

- Dr. Joan Vickers, instructional design expert,
- Dr. Rainer Martens, Publisher,
- the staff of Human Kinetics Publishers, and

- the *many* students, teachers, coaches, consultants, teacher educators, specialists, and administrators who shared their ideas—and dreams.

Judy Patterson Wright
Series Editor

Preface

When I was approached as a potential author for this book, I wondered, ''Why me?'' Then, looking back, I realized that swimming has more profoundly influenced my life than any other activity. So much satisfaction results from being one with—being at home in—the water that swimming has become for me the most wholesome, relaxing, invigorating, confidence-building activity imaginable, and it is a skill that gives one life-saving ability in a water emergency.

I want in this book to simplify for beginning swimmers what is usually perceived to be a complex, difficult process. My experience with traditional methods of teaching swimming and with their limitations motivated me to produce a course with a different approach. The uniqueness of this approach to teaching swimming is its basic premise, one often overlooked by instructors who believe one must ''swim to stay up''—swimming is easy! So easy that it can be accomplished with less effort than is needed for any other physical sport. The emphasis in the approach taught here is on ease and relaxation; not on ''kick-kick-kick''

or ''pull-pull-pull,'' which exhausts the novice so quickly.

If you follow the precepts of this book, you will be led gently into a new and fascinating activity. If you are not careful, it may captivate you, too, and may even change your life. CAUTION! It may be habit-forming!

I would like to acknowledge the contributions of my many hundreds of students, who have taught me all I know about swimming, and I dedicate this book to each person who has ever said to me, ''I took some swimming lessons once, but I just couldn't learn.'' I am grateful for the help and guidance of Dr. Judy Patterson Wright, who has had confidence in my ability to teach you to swim. Dr. Patterson Wright has guided me into the research-oriented teaching methods needed for this text.

I also acknowledge with awe the talents of the artists who took ordinary photos and transformed them into clear and superior teaching and learning tools.

David G. Thomas

The Steps to Success Staircase

Get ready to climb a staircase—one that will lead you to be a great swimmer. You cannot leap to the top; you get there by climbing one step at a time.

Each of the 24 steps you will take is an easy transition from the one before. The first few steps of the staircase provide a foundation—a solid foundation of basic skills and concepts. As you progress further, you will learn how to connect groups of those seemingly isolated skills. Practicing common combinations of swimming skills will give you the experience you need to begin making natural and accurate decisions in the water. You will learn to choose the proper stroke to match your various swimming needs—whether speed, ease, distance, or fun. As you near the top of the staircase, the climb will ease, and you'll find that you have developed a sense of confidence in your swimming ability that makes further progress a real joy.

To prepare to become a good climber, familiarize yourself with this section, as well as the "Swimming" and "Preparing Your Body for Success" sections for an orientation and in order to understand how to set up your practice sessions around the steps.

Follow the same sequence each step of the way:

1. Read the explanations of what is covered in the step, why the step is important, and how to execute or perform the step's focus, which may be on basic skills, concepts, tactics, or some combination of the three.
2. Follow the numbered illustrations showing exactly how to position your body to execute each basic skill successfully. There are three general parts to each skill: preparation (getting into a starting position), execution (performing the skill that is the focus of the step), and follow-through (recovering to starting position).
3. Look over the common errors that may occur and the recommendations for how to correct them.
4. Read the directions and the Success Goal for each drill. Practice accordingly and record your scores. Compare your score with the Success Goal for the drill. You need to meet the Success Goal of each drill before moving on to practice the next one, because the drills are arranged in an easy-to-difficult progression. This sequence is designed specifically to help you achieve continual success. The drills help you improve your skills through repetition and purposeful practice.
5. As soon as you can reach all the Success Goals for one step, you are ready for a qualified observer—such as your teacher, coach, or trained partner—to evaluate your basic skill technique against the Keys to Success Checklist. This is a qualitative or subjective evaluation of your basic technique or form, because using correct form can enhance your performance. Your evaluator can tailor specific goals for you, if they are needed, by using the Individual Program Sheet (see the Appendix).
6. Repeat these procedures for each of the 24 Steps to Success. Then rate yourself according to the directions in the "Rating Your Total Progress" section.

Good luck on your step-by-step journey to developing your swimming skills, building confidence, experiencing success, and having fun!

Swimming

In ancient times people took to the water to avoid forest fires, to escape enemies, to search for food, or simply for relief from the blazing sun. Besides such practical reasons, humankind has been attracted to the water by an unexplainable force through the ages. Children seek puddles to play in. Sailors are irresistibly drawn to the sea. Vacationers flock to the seaside for the soothing sights and sounds of the water. The ancient Japanese, observing its effect on people, identified water as "the source of all wisdom" in the samurai code.

The ability to be one with the water and to take pleasure in the weightless freedom it provides is a never-ending source of enjoyment. It provides amusement, relaxation, challenge, competition, and a means of saving your life in an emergency. The old and well-used axiom is as true today as when it was coined: "You can't find a better sport to save your life" (attributed to Commodore Wilbur Longfellow of the American Red Cross).

Learning to swim well is the first phase of attaining real water ease and skill. Swimming has no rules that must be followed, other than the natural laws of buoyancy and propulsion (and rules for competition, of course). You can swim in any manner or position, with as much or as little energy expenditure as you wish to invest, and at any age.

There are, however, certain combinations of motions that have proven to be more efficient than others for certain purposes. These efficient motions have been "packaged" into recognized strokes. The best known of these strokes are the crawl, the breaststroke, the back crawl, the elementary backstroke, the sidestroke, and the butterfly.

There are no rules for the crawl, sidestroke, or the elementary backstroke. Each stroke is correctly swum whenever it is yielding the greatest efficiency. Rules for the other strokes have been established because they are used in competition and must be governed by rules to ensure fairness. The crawl is also used in competition, but it is used under the heading of *Freestyle*, which allows any form of movement; therefore, it is not governed by rules.

This book will enable you to learn four very different stroke packages: the crawl, which is the fastest and most efficient stroke known; the elementary backstroke, which is the easiest and safest stroke and the one most useful for conservation of energy; the sidestroke, which is used for lifesaving; and the breaststroke, which is the "social" or "conversational" stroke. There are several other stroke packages that are not so widely practiced and come with advanced water expertise, along with hundreds of other skills, stunts, figures, and games. You will want to continue your progress by learning many of these strokes and skills that are beyond the scope of this book.

SWIMMING TODAY

The field of water safety is a growing field that offers challenges to anyone who wishes to make a career of aquatics. Leadership positions in lifeguarding, swim instruction, and swim facility operation and management are constantly changing as the sport of swimming expands. This book is your starting point. If your interest lies in swim instruction, or lifesaving and lifeguarding, you will want to be familiar with the programs of the American Red Cross and the YMCA.

If competition is your forte, you will want to become involved in speed swimming through such ruling organizations as U.S. Swimming, the National Collegiate Athletic Association, or the National Interscholastic Swimming Association. Competition in aquatics could also lead you to water polo (U.S. Water Polo); synchronized swimming (U.S. Synchro); underwater hockey (National Underwater Hockey Association); springboard diving (U.S. Diving); competitive lifesaving (National Surf Lifesaving Association); fin swimming (Underwater Society of America); and scuba diving (National Association of

Underwater Instructors, Professional Association of Diving Instructors, the YMCA, National Association of Scuba Diving Schools, and others).

Basic swimming—the root of all of these activities—is taught right here in this book. The skills you'll learn here are the beginning for every area in the fascinating world of aquatics.

SAFETY RULES

The dangers inherent in entering the water demand that certain personal rules of conduct be observed for the safety of aquatic participants. Some of the most important follow:

- Never swim alone. Always have with you someone who can help, or can get help, in an emergency.
- Know the area where you plan to swim. Know where the deep and shallow areas are and find out about any hidden hazards that are not apparent from above the water.
- Never swim immediately after a heavy meal. Wait at least 30 minutes after a light meal and longer after a heavy meal.
- Never chew gum while swimming. Breathing patterns in swimming require a clear mouth and throat.
- Do not run, push, or indulge in horseplay on a pool deck. The area is usually wet and slippery, and accidents can easily happen.
- For sanitary reasons every health department requires each person to shower before entering a pool.
- Health departments also prohibit any food or drink in a pool area.

EQUIPMENT

The following items of equipment will be used in Swimming: Steps to Success:

- Kickboard
- Leg float
- Face mask
- Swim fins
- Snorkel

- "Deep float" leg float
- Float belt
- Hula hoop

Kickboards and leg floats are standard equipment at most pools. You may be permitted to use them, or you can buy your own inexpensively. The next three items—face mask, swim fins, and snorkel—are personal fit items. You will want to supply your own for fit and for personal hygiene. Masks and fins are the most expensive items; fins are not absolutely essential in completing the Swimming: Steps to Success, but they are of considerable value. The deep float leg float, float belt, and hula hoop are very easy and inexpensive to make yourself. (You will not need a float belt unless you are male and totally nonbuoyant; only one in 20 males is so nonbuoyant.)

Make a "deep float" leg support by tying a piece of light line to the handle of an empty half-gallon plastic container with a good waterproof top, such as a milk, juice, or cider container. Make the line long enough so that a 4-inch loop in the end of the line will hang 12 inches underwater when the container is floating. You use this float by inserting one ankle into the loop. This allows you to have some leg support at a depth of about 1 foot for some of your swimming drills (starting with Step 11).

A float belt can be made by cutting blocks of closed-cell plastic foam, such as polyethylene, about 2 inches square and 6 to 8 inches long. Each of these blocks (you may need 4 or 6 of them) should be slit so that a 2-inch-wide webbed nylon belt can be passed through them. A belt of the type scuba divers use for a weight belt is ideal. (If you need a float belt, it will be used in the first three steps.)

The hula hoop is a ring, usually made of rigid 1-inch plastic tubing. It can be purchased in many toy stores. It must float. If it is plastic tubing, you may wish to seal the joint where the ends meet, so as to make it watertight. Attach a small weight to one point on the ring so that when immersed, it stands on edge on the bottom of the pool. (It will be used for diving in Steps 22 and 24.)

Preparing Your Body for Success

There is a recommended swimming workout sequence to follow. Prior to practicing, you need a 5- to 10-minute warm-up period to aid in increasing your lung capacity and endurance and to increase your body's flexibility. After finishing a practice, end with a 5-minute taper period to stretch and relax the muscles you have used. If you follow this sequence, you will prepare your body and mind to swim, and you will be relaxed and at ease afterward.

A TWO-PHASE WARM-UP PERIOD

Your first goal is to complete both breathing exercises described below, which review breathing techniques and increase your lung capacity. Then perform one flexibility exercise per body part listed under "Flexibility Exercises." You will become mentally and physically prepared for swimming.

Breathing Exercises

1. Stand erect with your feet spread and your arms at your sides. Inhale deeply while lifting your arms laterally overhead to full extension. Exhale slowly while your arms return to your sides. Repeat 5 times.

2. Inhale quickly; hold your breath while your arms are lifted and lowered slowly. When your arms have returned to your sides, exhale and inhale *very* quickly through your mouth, making sure to take in all the air you can hold. Repeat this quick exhale/inhale-and-hold cycle 5 times, using only your mouth for breathing; raise and lower your arms each time.

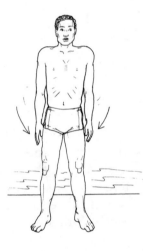

Flexibility Exercises

Concentrate on your body as you perform the following exercises (if necessary, close your eyes to avoid distraction and to focus attention on your body). Select **one** exercise for each body part. Stretch until you feel mild tension. Avoid comparing your stretch to anyone else's.

Head

1. Lie on your stomach. Place your hands to support your head. Turn your head to the right, relax, and slowly count to 30. Turn your head to the left, relax, and slowly count to 30. Repeat both sides 3 times.

2. Sitting or standing, let your head tilt to your right shoulder. Do a slow half-circle, dropping your head forward and over to your left shoulder, while counting to 8. (Do not drop your head back—this movement can put too much pressure on the bones of the neck.) Do 3 right half-circles and 3 left half-circles.

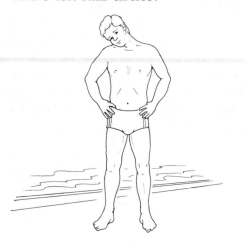

Arms

1. Standing or sitting, interlock your fingers, turn your palms toward the ceiling, and stretch both arms over your head. Hold this position for 20–30 seconds, your head remaining facing forward. Repeat 3 times.

2. Standing with your arms out at shoulder height, circle your arms in small, tight circles forward 10 times, then backward 10 times. Next, slowly do 10 forward arm

circles using small, then gradually larger, circles. Reverse direction and make 10 gradually larger circles backward. Repeat 3 times.

Torso

1. Standing or sitting, lift your left arm toward the ceiling and over to one side. Keep your hips and shoulders square to the front to stretch your side muscles, not your back muscles. Hold for 20–30 seconds. Now do this stretch with your right arm. Repeat both sides 3 times.

2. Standing or sitting, shrug both your shoulders up toward your ears. Roll your shoulders forward in a slow, circular motion while counting to 8. Roll your shoulders backward. Repeat 3 times in both directions.

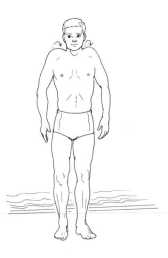

Legs

1. Sit with your legs out straight and your toes pointed away from your body. Lean your chest over your knees and reach gently toward your ankles with ankles flexed. Do not bounce. Hold for 20–30 seconds. Do the same stretch with your toes pointed. Repeat both stretch positions 3 times.

2. Start in the lunge position; your hands balancing you in front, your left knee bent, right knee facing the ground, and both toes flexed. Slowly lower your body into a deeper lunge. Hold for 20–30 seconds. Repeat both sides 3 times.

Feet

1. Sitting or standing, circle your right ankle clockwise 8 times, then counterclockwise 8 times. Repeat with your left ankle.

2. Stand 1–2 1/2 feet from a wall, and place both hands against the wall. Keep your body in a straight line, and slowly lean forward to stretch your achilles tendons. Hold for 20–30 seconds. Repeat 3 times.

COOL-DOWN PERIOD

1. Standing in shoulder-deep water, stretch both of your arms overhead. Hold them stretched as you take a very deep breath. Hold for 5 seconds and exhale slowly. Relax. Repeat 4 times.

2. Standing in chin-deep water, your arms out to the sides, lay your head back until your ears are underwater. Leave your heels on the pool bottom, take a deep breath, and slowly arch your back to a heels-down back float position. Close your eyes. Exhale and inhale quickly, but hold each breath for 5 seconds. Take a full minute to consciously relax, in turn, your neck muscles, shoulder muscles, arm muscles, and, finally, your legs.

Step 1 Buoyancy

Swimming may be defined as floating while propelling your body from one point to another. Basic to all swimming is the fact that your body is lighter than water and floats (one adult male in 20 needs to make small hand motions to keep floating, though). Buoyancy—this tendency to float or rise when submerged—is an inherent body characteristic and need not be learned.

This step teaches you how to discover this fact for yourself and how to control the natural buoyancy of your body to make it work for you. Control of your buoyancy involves 4 elements:

- Control of the *amount* of buoyancy through breath control
- Control of your body position through balance
- Relaxation
- Recovery to a standing position

HOW TO PROVE THAT *YOUR* BODY FLOATS

For your safety and peace of mind, **ALWAYS** have an instructor or friend standing beside you while you attempt a new skill.

Human bodies do not float *on* the water—they float *in* it! Only a certain percentage of your body will remain above the surface; this percentage varies with every person. To discover what amount of your body remains above the water surface, find a place at the edge of the pool where the water is chin-deep. Hold onto the side with two fingers of each hand, keeping your stomach tight against the wall. Take a big breath until your lungs are totally filled. Hold that breath, bend your knees so your feet are off the bottom, look straight forward (do not tilt your head back), and lower yourself *slowly* until only the very top of your head is above water. Bring both hands under the water momentarily. YOU ARE FLOATING!

Take hold of the edge and stand again (see Figure 1.1).

Figure 1.1 Keys to Success: *Buoyancy*

**Preparation
Phase**

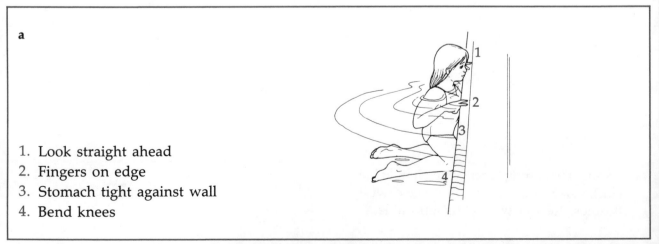

1. Look straight ahead
2. Fingers on edge
3. Stomach tight against wall
4. Bend knees

Execution Phase

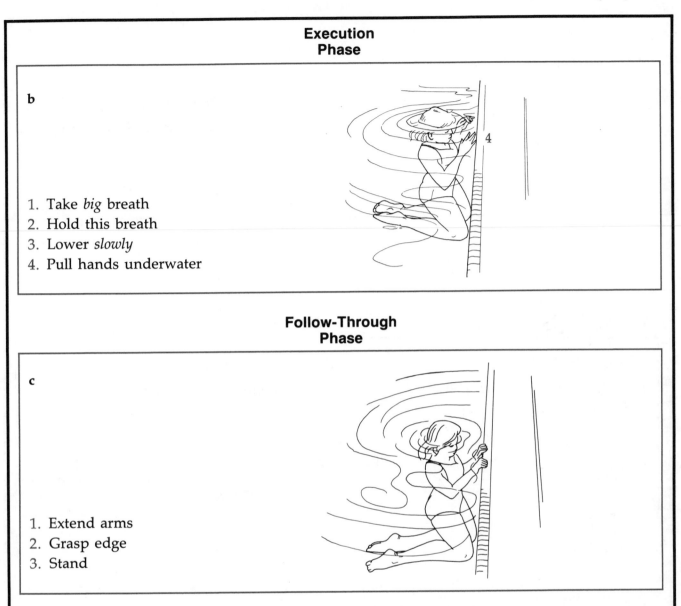

b

1. Take *big* breath
2. Hold this breath
3. Lower *slowly*
4. Pull hands underwater

Follow-Through Phase

c

1. Extend arms
2. Grasp edge
3. Stand

Note: For those few adult males who have neutral or negative buoyancy: It is suggested that you ask your teacher to fit you with a solid foam buoyancy belt that gives you enough positive buoyancy to float at eye-level in this exercise. The belt should be attached under the armpits, and the buoyancy should be circumferential, or distributed equally around the body. You should wear the belt until you have completed Step 3.

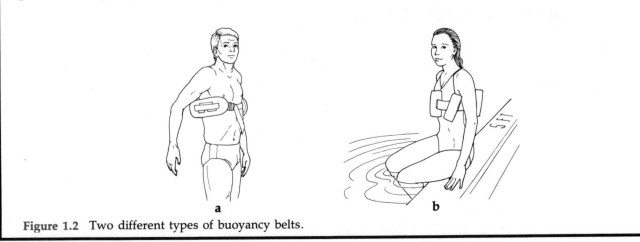

a   b

Figure 1.2 Two different types of buoyancy belts.

Detecting Errors in Floating Technique

Learning to float is easier if you can compare correct techniques with incorrect techniques. The most common floating errors are listed below, along with suggestions on how to correct them.

ERROR    **CORRECTION**

ERROR	CORRECTION
1. Head tilts back.	1. Look straight forward.
2. Body drifts away from wall.	2. Keep elbows tightly bent.
3. Head drops beneath surface.	3. Lower your body *very* slowly.
4. Head continues to sink.	4. Take and hold *all the air you can*.
5. Correct technique used, but body still sinks.	5. One adult male in 20 cannot float motionless. Use a buoyancy belt temporarily (see Figure 1.2).

Buoyancy Drills

1. Buoyancy Discovery Drill

Repeat the exercise described in Figure 1.1 several times. Try it both with eyes closed and with eyes open.

Success Goal = 5 vertical floats with full confidence that your body will not sink and with some degree of relaxation

Your Score = (#) _____ vertical floats with full confidence

2. Deep-Water Buoyancy Discovery Drill

With an instructor in the water with you, repeat in deep water the exercise described in Figure 1.1. Keep your knees straight, though.

Success Goal = 5 repetitions in deep water with confidence and relaxation, holding each float for 15 seconds

Your Score = (#) _____ repetitions holding each for 15 seconds

Buoyancy
Keys to Success Checklist

You have been testing yourself objectively by performing a certain number of repetitions—a *quantitative* measure—in each of the Step 1 Success Goals. Next ask your teacher, coach, or a trained observer to evaluate the quality of your technique subjectively—assessing your floating *qualitatively*—according to the checklist below. He or she may decide to create an individual practice program to strengthen your weak spots.

Preparation Phase

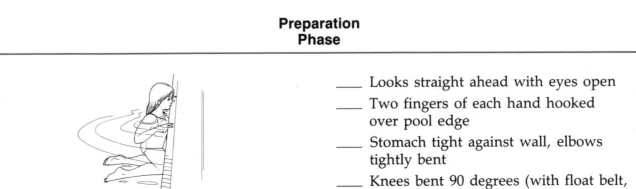

_____ Looks straight ahead with eyes open

_____ Two fingers of each hand hooked over pool edge

_____ Stomach tight against wall, elbows tightly bent

_____ Knees bent 90 degrees (with float belt, if necessary)

Execution
Phase

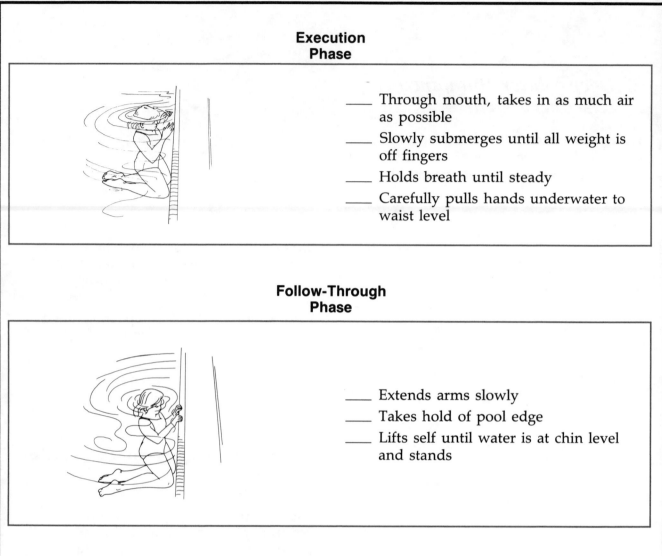

_____ Through mouth, takes in as much air as possible

_____ Slowly submerges until all weight is off fingers

_____ Holds breath until steady

_____ Carefully pulls hands underwater to waist level

Follow-Through
Phase

_____ Extends arms slowly

_____ Takes hold of pool edge

_____ Lifts self until water is at chin level and stands

Step 2 Back Float

Now that you know your body is buoyant, the next step is to be able to control this buoyancy to produce a body position that allows you to breathe while floating. Most beginners attempt to float in a horizontal position and feel threatened when their legs drop to a natural, balanced back float position, which is semivertical for most people.

WHY IS THE BACK FLOAT IMPORTANT?

The back float is one of the most important skills you will ever learn in swimming. It allows you to rest and breathe while floating. It requires almost no effort. It may save your life in the event of an aquatic emergency. It also teaches you how to balance your body in any position from vertical to horizontal.

HOW TO EXECUTE A BACK FLOAT

In chin-deep water, assume the same starting position at pool's edge as for the float in the previous step. However, now turn your face up to the ceiling and extend your arms fully, straightening your elbows, while still grasping the edge.

Be sure that your ears are fully submerged. Take a deep breath, release the edge, and bring your hands underwater. Keep your eyes open as you slowly drift backward away from the wall. (Continue to wear a float belt through this step if absolutely necessary. Position it as close as possible to lung position, split into two side floats.)

When steady in the water, *very quickly* exhale and inhale once through your mouth. Take in a *full* breath. Hold this breath for 5 seconds, then get another one. Remain perfectly still. Allow your knees to straighten. When you are confident, relax. Slowly bring your arms outward underwater until they are at shoulder height and stop. Then, keeping them fully submerged, continue to extend your arms beyond your head. Your feet will rise as your arms move up.

To recover, bring your knees up, drop your chin forward, and sweep your arms downward behind you and forward past your hips, palms forward (pushing the water forward with your palms like this swings your body back to the vertical). Hold still until your feet are under you, then stand (see Figure 2.1).

Figure 2.1 Keys to Success: *Back Float*

Preparation Phase

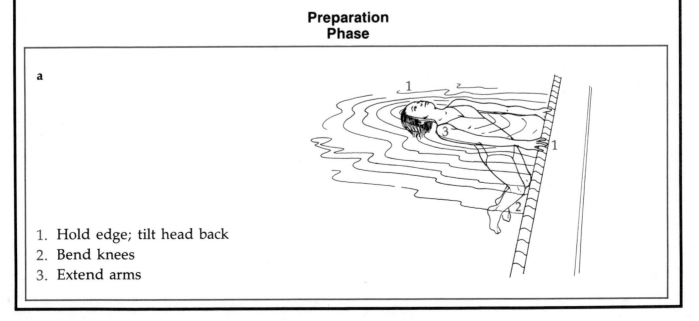

a

1. Hold edge; tilt head back
2. Bend knees
3. Extend arms

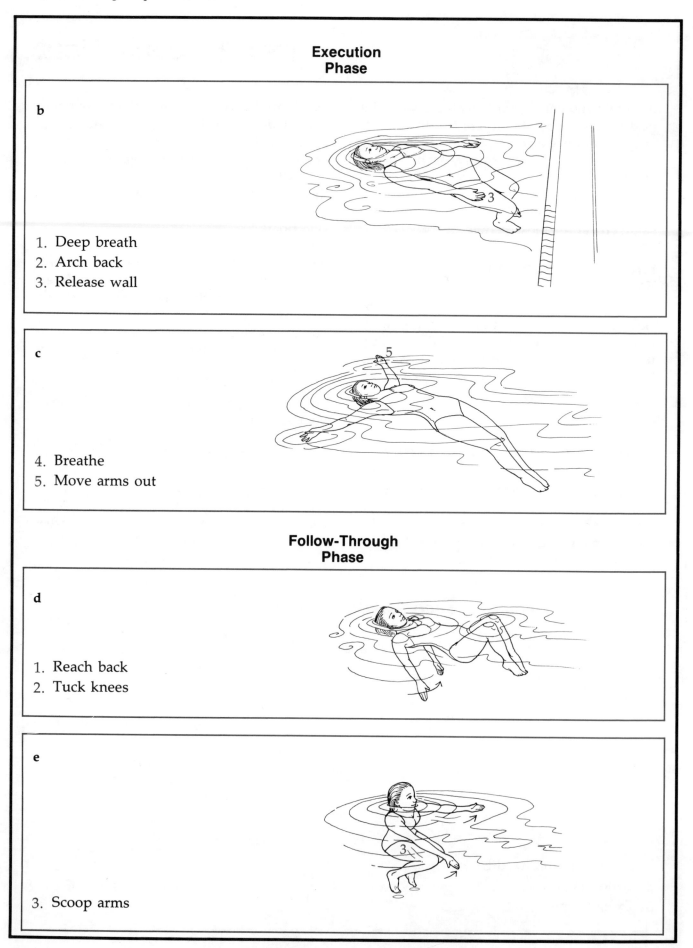

**Execution
Phase**

b

1. Deep breath
2. Arch back
3. Release wall

c

4. Breathe
5. Move arms out

**Follow-Through
Phase**

d

1. Reach back
2. Tuck knees

e

3. Scoop arms

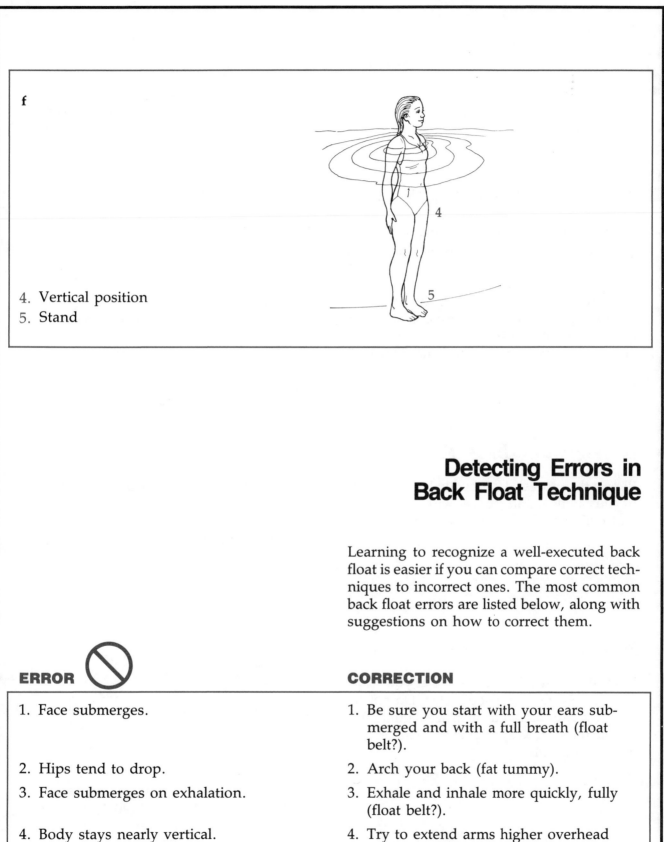

f

4. Vertical position
5. Stand

Detecting Errors in Back Float Technique

Learning to recognize a well-executed back float is easier if you can compare correct techniques to incorrect ones. The most common back float errors are listed below, along with suggestions on how to correct them.

ERROR ⃠	CORRECTION
1. Face submerges.	1. Be sure you start with your ears submerged and with a full breath (float belt?).
2. Hips tend to drop.	2. Arch your back (fat tummy).
3. Face submerges on exhalation.	3. Exhale and inhale more quickly, fully (float belt?).
4. Body stays nearly vertical.	4. Try to extend arms higher overhead without bringing them out of the water.
5. You have muscle fatigue.	5. Relax—no effort required!
6. You are breathless.	6. Breathe more often.

Back Float Drills

1. Land Drill on Breathing

Practice correct breathing techniques. Opening your mouth wide, take in all the air you can. Hold for just 5 seconds. Then exhale and inhale once as quickly as possible through your mouth, making sure that you get *all* the air you can. Hold for only 5 seconds, then exhale and inhale *quickly* again. Continue. See how quickly you can get each new breath.

Success Goal = 20 breaths held only 5 seconds each and taken very quickly without leaving you breathless

Your Score = (#) _____ breaths taken quickly and consecutively

2. Beginning Back Float Drill

Repeat the process described in Figure 2.1 until you can float and recover with confidence, and without submerging on the recovery.

Success Goal = 5 consecutive floats and recoveries without submerging

Your Score = (#) _____ consecutive floats and recoveries

3. Deep-Water Back Float

With an instructor in the water at your side, try the back float in deep water. Do not try to recover, but let your instructor guide you back to the side. Keep your eyes open. Breathe quickly, but fully.

Success Goal = 3 repetitions in deep water, holding float and breathing for 30 seconds each time

Your Score = (#) _____ seconds floating

4. Back Float From Standing Position

In chin-deep water, stand on the pool bottom, your arms out at shoulder height, palms up. Tilt your head back, your ears underwater. Take a deep breath, arch your back, and drift back into floating position. Do not try to lift your heels from the bottom. When floating, move your arms slowly overhead. Take a breath; hold as long as comfortable. Recover.

Success Goal = without your face submerging, 3 successive floats and recoveries for 2 full minutes

Your Score = (#) _____ seconds floating

Back Float Keys to Success Checklist

Attaining each of the Step 2 Success Goals measures your progress quantitatively. Quality is also important. The ease and confidence with which you perform a skill are evident to a trained observer. Ask your teacher or someone else with a trained eye to check the items listed below for the quality of your performance and to indicate items that need more attention in order to improve the overall quality of your back float.

Preparation Phase

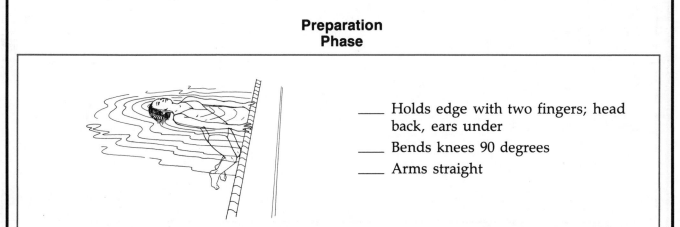

_____ Holds edge with two fingers; head back, ears under

_____ Bends knees 90 degrees

_____ Arms straight

Execution
Phase

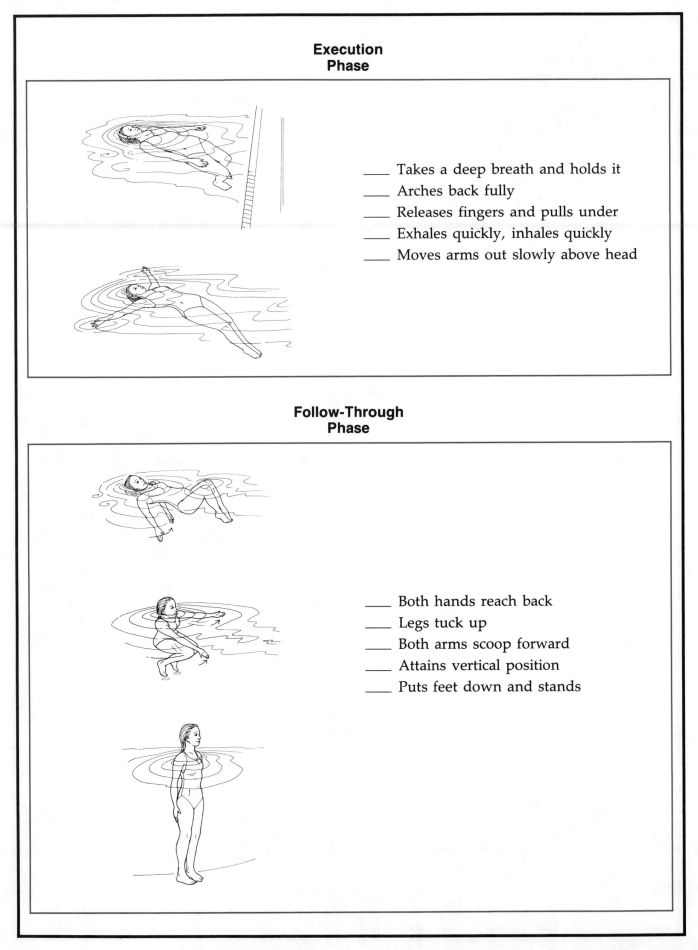

_____ Takes a deep breath and holds it
_____ Arches back fully
_____ Releases fingers and pulls under
_____ Exhales quickly, inhales quickly
_____ Moves arms out slowly above head

Follow-Through
Phase

_____ Both hands reach back
_____ Legs tuck up
_____ Both arms scoop forward
_____ Attains vertical position
_____ Puts feet down and stands

Step 3 Sculling

Sculling is an arm and hand motion that propels you through the water in a back floating position. It can also provide downward thrust to keep you at the surface. The few adult males who are not buoyant *must* use sculling to keep their faces free of the water when floating on their backs (they should try to do without their float belts after a few sculling practices).

WHY IS SCULLING IMPORTANT?

Swimming is moving from point to point while floating. Sculling is important because it is the first propulsive swimming movement you will learn. It is vital to those with very little buoyancy, because they would not be able to remain on the surface without it. Sculling is also the basis for all synchronized swimming figures and stunts. It is used in some manner by all swimmers at various times and greatly increases a swimmer's proficiency.

HOW TO EXECUTE SCULLING

Start from a back float position, your arms a few inches underwater along your sides. Bend your wrists slightly back. Keep your fingers together. Turn the heels of your hands outward and move your hands away from your body about 18 inches. Then turn the heels of your hands inward and move your hands back to the starting position. Continue this inward and outward movement without pause. This motion is exactly like polishing a vertical wall with your hands while your body is perpendicular to the wall (see Figure 3.1). (Note: Nonbuoyant persons must hold their wrists nearly straight to also apply downward pressure on the water.)

Figure 3.1 Keys to Success: *Sculling*

**Preparation
Phase**

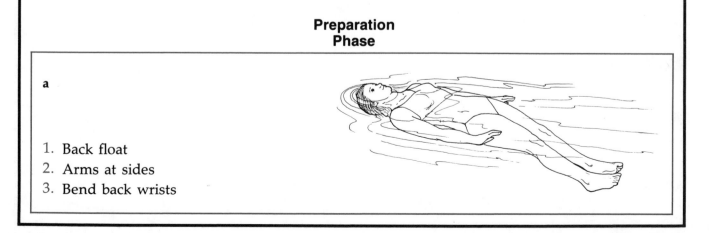

a

1. Back float
2. Arms at sides
3. Bend back wrists

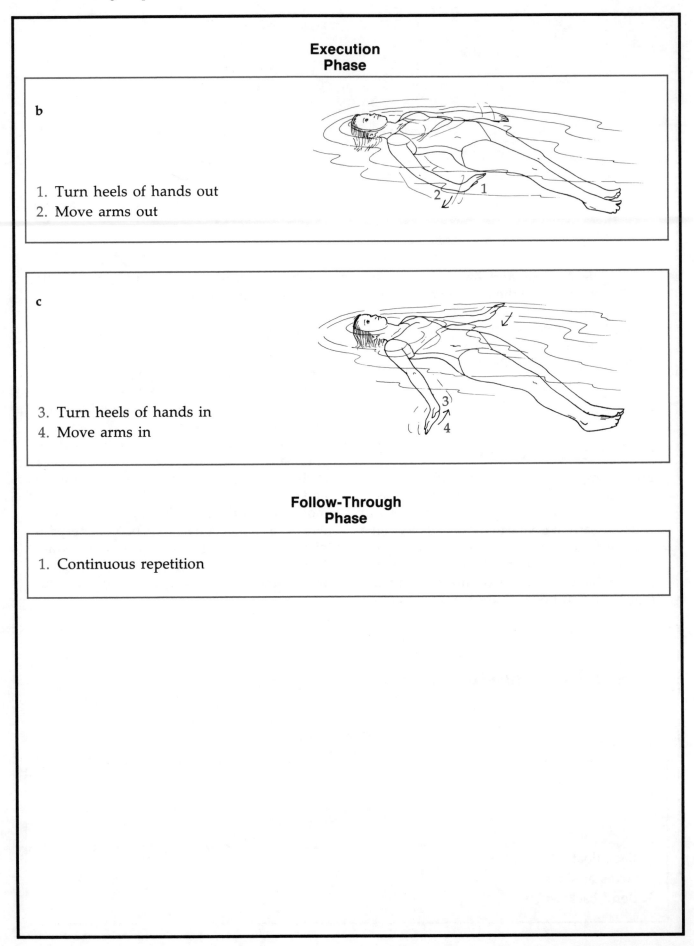

**Execution
Phase**

b

1. Turn heels of hands out
2. Move arms out

c

3. Turn heels of hands in
4. Move arms in

**Follow-Through
Phase**

1. Continuous repetition

Detecting Errors in Sculling Technique

Learning to recognize a well-executed sculling motion is easier if you can compare incorrect motions with correct ones. The most common sculling errors are listed below, along with suggestions on how to correct them.

ERROR 🚫	CORRECTION
1. You sink.	1. Take deeper breaths and hold each for 5 seconds.
2. You still sink.	2. Bend less at wrist. Keep fingers tight together. Maintain steady down pressure, avoiding up-down motions.
3. Legs stay down.	3. Scull forward faster.
4. Arms and hands tire.	4. Relax wrists and elbows.
5. No forward motion made.	5. Bend wrists more. Twist arms more.

Sculling Drills

1. Variations on Sculling

Scull for distance—do not try for speed. Practice making the sculling motions wider, then practice making them narrower.

Success Goal = 45 feet or across width of pool

Your Score = (#) _____ feet

2. Deep-Water Sculling

With an instructor, start in deep water and scull into shallow water. Scull for distance.

Success Goal = 75 feet or pool length

Your Score = (#) _____ feet

3. Scull and Turn Drill

In shallow water, start to scull, then hold one arm still. Scull with only one arm. You will discover that you will turn in the direction away from the sculling arm. Continue to turn a full circle.

Success Goal = 2 full circles in each direction

Your Score = (#) _____ circles in each direction

4. Deep-Water Scull and Turn Drill

With your instructor watching, start in shallow water a few feet from deep water. Scull into deep water. Stop sculling with one arm and turn until you are heading back into shallow water. Scull again with both arms until you are once more in shallow water. Turn in the other direction and repeat.

Success Goal = 5 turns in each direction

Your Score = (#) _____ turns

5. Sculling With Handicap Drill

In shallow water, wear a weight belt and scull across the pool.

Success Goal = 6 pounds across pool

Your Score = (#) _____ pounds

6. Sculling for Speed Drill

In shallow water, race your classmates.

(No goal, no score.)

Sculling
Keys to Success Checklist

Sculling is so important to your swimming that you need an evaluation of your progress based not only on quantitative (numerically measurable) aspects but also on qualitative aspects. For instance, in sculling, the ''feel'' for the pressure of water on the hand is very important to learn. A person with a trained eye can look at your sculling and see to what extent you have mastered this aspect. Ask your teacher or another expert in sculling to evaluate your skill qualitatively. The checklist below allows him or her to select areas that may need special attention to make your sculling high quality.

Preparation Phase

___ Floats on back
___ Arms barely underwater at sides
___ Bends wrists back comfortably

Execution Phase

___ Arm rotates so heel of hand is pointed out
___ Arms move outward about 18 inches
___ Smooth transition from outward movement through rotation of arm and hand, so heel of hand faces inward
___ Smooth inward motion and rotation

Follow-Through Phase

___ Continuous figure 8 hand motion

Step 4 Elementary Backstroke Arm Motion

Again, swimming is a process of moving from one point to another while floating. You have learned to move while floating, but only in a simple fashion. Some motions or combinations of motions are more efficient than others. These valuable combinations are "packaged" and given such names as the *crawl* and *breaststroke*. One very efficient combination of motions—the elementary backstroke—is quite easy to do.

WHY IS THE ELEMENTARY BACKSTROKE ARM MOTION IMPORTANT?

The elementary backstroke arm motion is the most restful of all the arm motions used in swimming. It propels you with considerable efficiency but also incorporates a long glide phase that allows you to rest between strokes. Many tired swimmers have used the elementary backstroke arm motion to save their lives when they were too fatigued to continue swimming any other stroke.

HOW TO PERFORM THE ELEMENTARY BACKSTROKE ARM MOTION

Start the elementary backstroke in the back float position with your arms along your sides. The recovery (here the preparation phase) is performed by sliding both of your thumbs upward along your thighs and beyond until your thumbs are touching the top of your shoulders, wrists fully flexed. Rotate your forearms until your fingertips point outward.

The execution phase starts with the "catch." Extend your arms, fingertips leading, slightly beyond shoulder level. Take hold of the water with your hands and arms. Think about fastening your hands to the water and pulling your body past your hands. Pull horizontally just under the surface from shoulders to thighs. If your pull is level, your arms will finish the pull slightly in front of your thighs.

The follow-through phase is a long glide in a streamlined back float position (see Figure 4.1).

Figure 4.1 Keys to Success: *Elementary Backstroke Arm Motion*

Preparation Phase

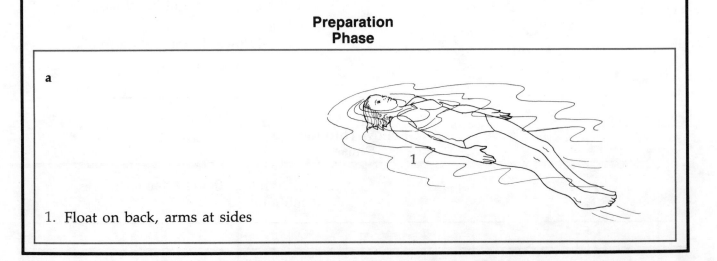

a

1. Float on back, arms at sides

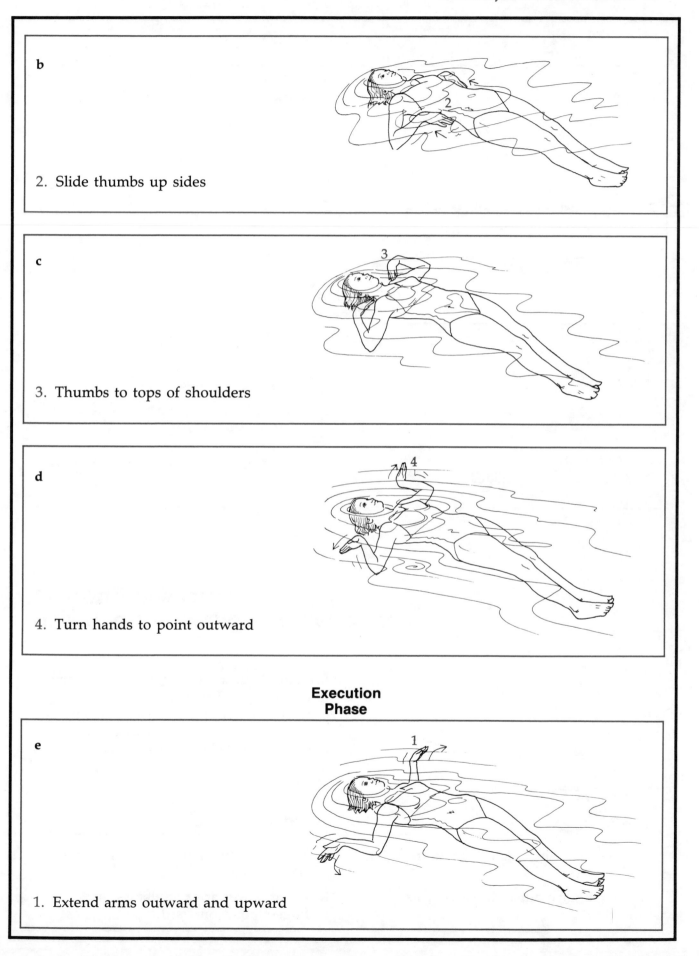

b

2. Slide thumbs up sides

c

3. Thumbs to tops of shoulders

d

4. Turn hands to point outward

**Execution
Phase**

e

1. Extend arms outward and upward

f

2. Stretch just above shoulder height
3. Pull horizontally toward feet

**Follow-Through
Phase**

g

1. Arms at side
2. Relax during long glide

Detecting Errors in
Elementary Backstroke Arm Motion

Learning to recognize a well-executed elementary backstroke arm motion is easier if you can compare correct and incorrect motions. The most common errors in backstroke arm motions are listed below, along with suggestions on how to correct them.

ERROR 🚫

CORRECTION

1. Hands start moving out before reaching shoulders.

2. Hands move out with backs of hands leading.

1. Keep thumbs tight to sides until hands reach shoulders.

2. Rotate lower arms at elbows until fingers point outward.

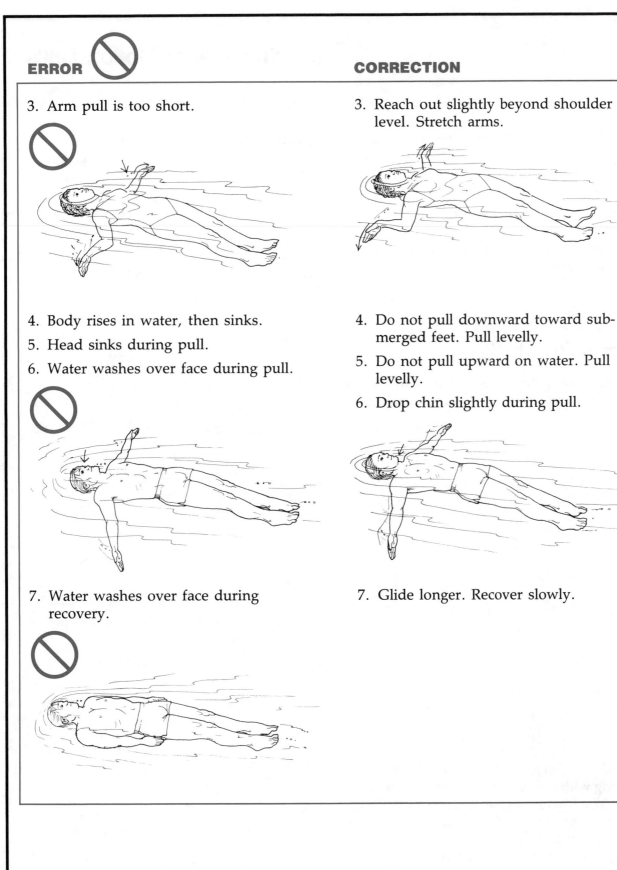

ERROR

3. Arm pull is too short.

4. Body rises in water, then sinks.
5. Head sinks during pull.
6. Water washes over face during pull.

7. Water washes over face during recovery.

CORRECTION

3. Reach out slightly beyond shoulder level. Stretch arms.

4. Do not pull downward toward submerged feet. Pull levelly.
5. Do not pull upward on water. Pull levelly.
6. Drop chin slightly during pull.

7. Glide longer. Recover slowly.

Backstroke Arm Motion Drills

1. Shallow-Water Drill

In shallow water, pull across pool. Count arm pulls necessary.

Success Goal = 5 feet per stroke

Your Score = (#) _____ feet per stroke

2. Deep-Water Drill

With your instructor watching, start in deep water and pull into shallow water.

Success Goal = 75 feet or one pool length

Your Score = (#) _____ feet

3. Backstroke and Sculling Drill

Start sculling. After 25 feet, change to backstroke arm motion, then return to sculling.

Success Goal = 4 successful transitions or one pool length

Your Score = (#) _____ transitions

4. Backstroke Pull and Turn Drill

In shallow water, start stroking. Then stop stroking with one arm and continue with the other. You will turn in the direction away from your pulling arm. Continue until you have made a complete circle. Repeat with your other arm, turning in the other direction.

Success Goal = 5 circles in each direction

Your Score = (#) _____ circles

5. Deep-Water Backstroke Turn Drill

With your instructor watching, start in shallow water a few feet from the deep section and pull into deep water. Then pull with only one arm until you are heading back into shallow water. Pull again with both arms until you are once again in shallow water.

Success Goal = 5 deep-water turns in each direction

Your Score = (#) _____ deep-water turns

6. Backstroke Distance Drill

With your instructor watching, start at the shallow end of the pool and pull all the way to the deep end (or 75 feet). Turn and pull all the way back to the shallow end (total: 150 feet).

Success Goal = 2 pool lengths or 150 feet

Your Score = (#) _____ feet

Elementary Backstroke Arm Motion Keys to Success Checklist

There is more to the elementary backstroke arm motion than the distance covered. The length of each pull and an awareness of the pressure exerted on the water are important factors that are not measured by the distance covered. Ask a person trained in teaching swimming to evaluate your arm stroke qualitatively and to use the checklist below to identify areas that need more work.

Preparation
Phase

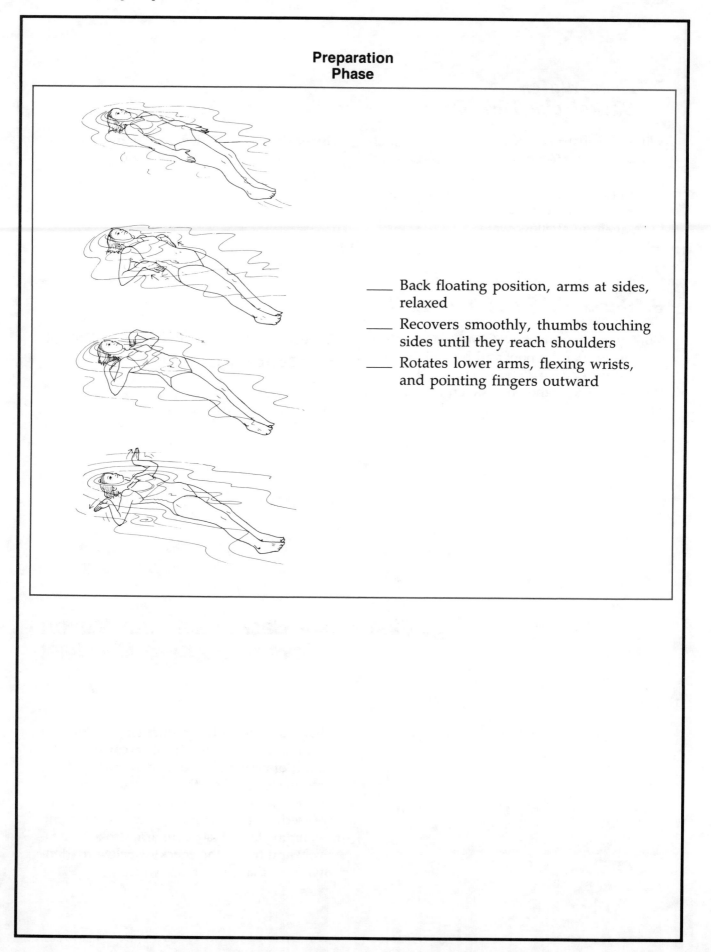

_____ Back floating position, arms at sides, relaxed

_____ Recovers smoothly, thumbs touching sides until they reach shoulders

_____ Rotates lower arms, flexing wrists, and pointing fingers outward

Execution
Phase

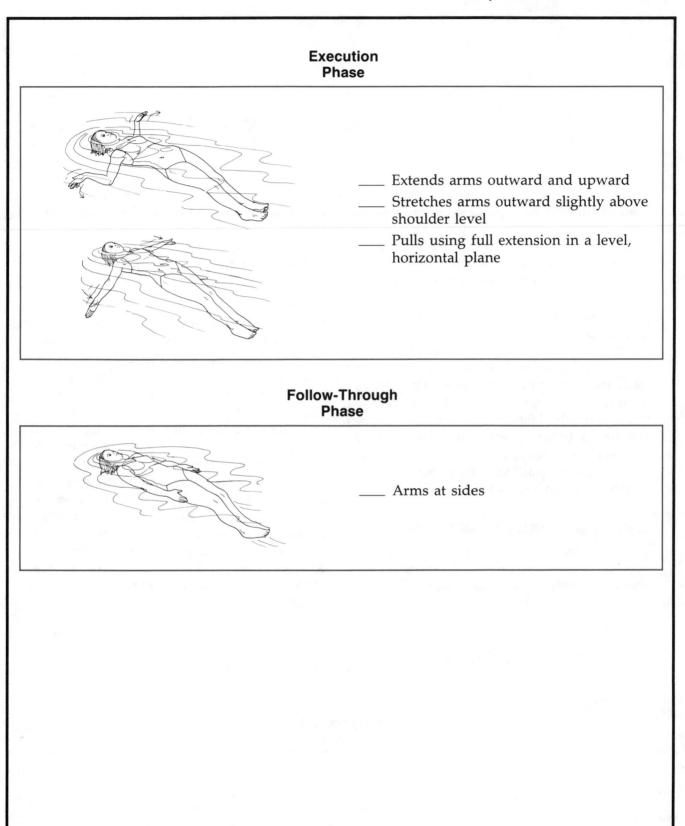

____ Extends arms outward and upward

____ Stretches arms outward slightly above shoulder level

____ Pulls using full extension in a level, horizontal plane

Follow-Through
Phase

____ Arms at sides

Step 5 **Support Kicking**

Three important functions are served by motions of the legs and feet in swimming: support, propulsion, and balance. The relative importance of these three functions varies greatly with the individual swimmer. Those who have buoyant legs need very little, if any, support from the leg and foot motion. Such persons may spend less time on this step and quickly go on to Step 6.

Kicking the legs also helps balance the body in such strokes as the crawl, in which the arms move independently of each other. Propulsion from the legs varies greatly with the type of kick and the flexibility of the swimmer's knees and ankles. In some strokes, the kick supplies a major proportion of the propulsion; in others, the propulsion gained may not be worth the effort expended.

WHY IS KICKING IMPORTANT?

For all swimmers and for all strokes, kicking supplies at least one of the functions described above. Therefore, it is important to learn proper methods of leg and ankle motion and the variations within a kick that aid in determining which of the functions will be maximized. At this stage, Step 5, we are more interested in support than in propulsion.

HOW TO KICK FOR SUPPORT

While sculling or stroking on your back, extend the toes of your right foot. Press downward on the water with the sole of this foot. Then draw your foot toward your body by bending your knee and hip. Just before your knee breaks the water surface, hook your toes and "step" up to the surface. Your left leg and foot perform the same motions in half-cycle opposition to your right leg. The result is *very* similar to pedaling a bicycle, with emphasis on "pressing the pedals" with your toes extended. Your foot should be hooked when moving upward and pointed when moving downward, pressing the water with the sole. Keep your feet and knees under the surface. No splash or surface waves should result (see Figure 5.1).

*Figure 5.1 Keys to Success: **Support Kicking***

**Preparation
Phase**

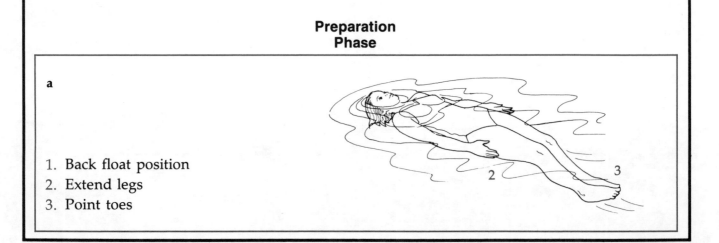

a

1. Back float position
2. Extend legs
3. Point toes

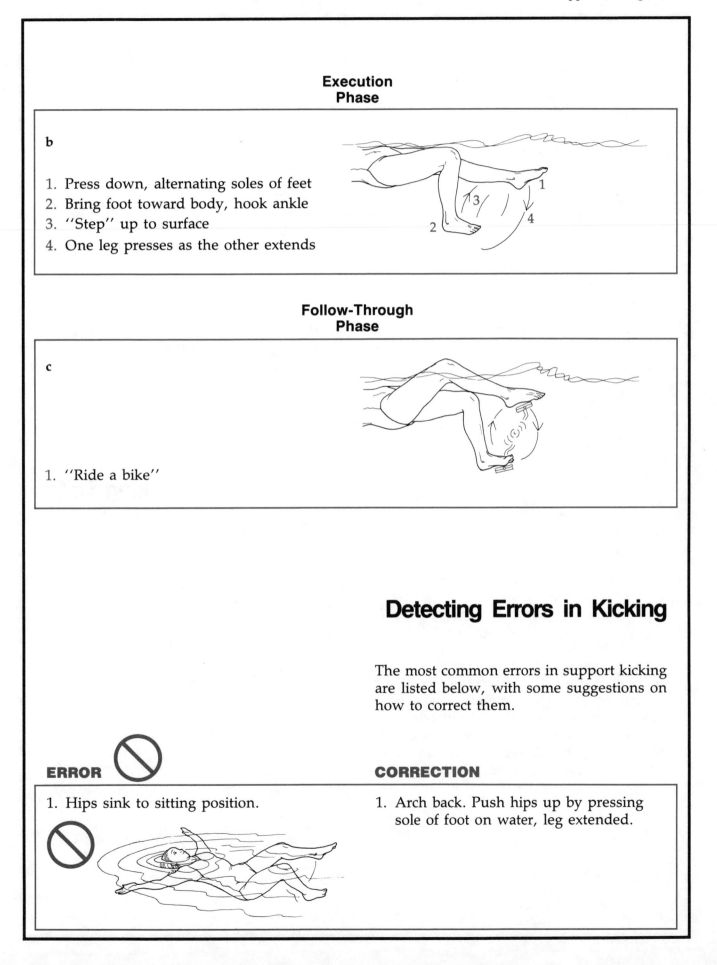

**Execution
Phase**

b

1. Press down, alternating soles of feet
2. Bring foot toward body, hook ankle
3. "Step" up to surface
4. One leg presses as the other extends

**Follow-Through
Phase**

c

1. "Ride a bike"

Detecting Errors in Kicking

The most common errors in support kicking are listed below, with some suggestions on how to correct them.

ERROR

1. Hips sink to sitting position.

CORRECTION

1. Arch back. Push hips up by pressing sole of foot on water, leg extended.

ERROR  **CORRECTION**

2. Water splashes into face.	2. Do not allow knee or foot to break surface.
3. Legs sink while kicking.	3. Work ankle: point toes while pressing, hook foot while lifting.

Kicking Drills

1. Support Kick Bracket Drill

In shallow water, with your back against the pool wall, hook your elbows over the edge of the pool or into the overflow trough and bend at your hips. With your legs extended in front of you, start the support kick, with emphasis on the downward press. As you press each foot, try to arch your hips upward until they are at the surface. Keep your feet underwater.

Success Goal = hips up 5 times, for 1 minute each time

Your Score = (#) _____ times

2. Support Kick
With Kickboard Drill

In shallow water, hold a kickboard behind
your neck. Keep your back arched, hips up.
Using the support kick, step up to the surface.
Avoid dropping your hips into sitting position.
Keep your chin up.

Success Goal = 5 minutes sustained horizontal position (you will
discover that you also
moved forward, but that
is not the goal)

Your Score = (#) _____ minutes

3. Shallow-Water Support
Kick and Float Drill

Float in a back float position with your arms
at your sides. Begin the support kick and step
up to the surface. Continue to kick in this
position.

Success Goal = 5 minutes in back float
position

Your Score = (#) _____ minutes

4. Shallow-Water Support
Kick and Pull Drill

While floating, your arms outstretched, slowly
begin the support kick. Step up with the
hooked ankle and press with your toes extended. When your hips are near the surface,

begin propulsive arm motions, either sculling or stroking. Then stop all motion, breathe in *deeply*, and allow your legs to sink as you float with your arms extended overhead.

Success Goal = repeat the drill 5 times without your face submerging

Your Score = (#) _____ repetitions without submerging

5. Deep-Water Support Kick Drill

With your instructor watching, start floating on your back in deep water. Start the support kick and scull gently, turning as necessary to remain in deep water.

Success Goal = 5 minutes in deep water

Your Score = (#) _____ minutes

Support Kicking Keys to Success Checklist

You have been working on support kicking to achieve measurable, quantitative goals. Now it is time to ask your teacher or another qualified swim instructor to look at your support kick to determine its qualitative aspects. Support kicking should evolve into an easy, fluid motion that will serve its purpose without requiring much attention or effort. Ask your evaluator to use the following checklist to indicate which items, if any, need more attention to give you that ''quality swimmer'' look.

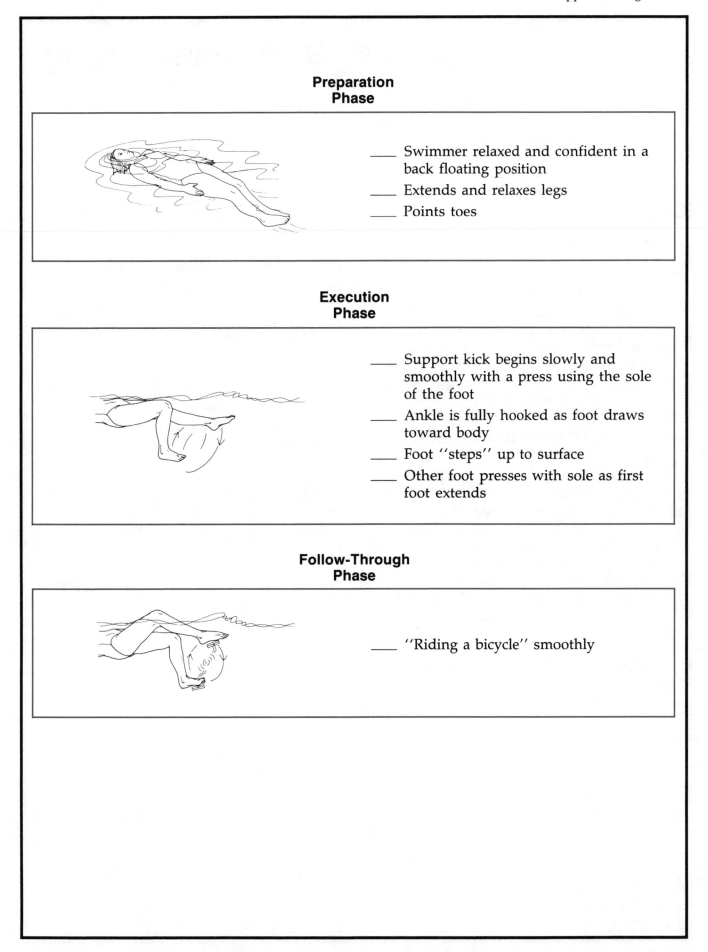

**Preparation
Phase**

___ Swimmer relaxed and confident in a back floating position

___ Extends and relaxes legs

___ Points toes

**Execution
Phase**

___ Support kick begins slowly and smoothly with a press using the sole of the foot

___ Ankle is fully hooked as foot draws toward body

___ Foot "steps" up to surface

___ Other foot presses with sole as first foot extends

**Follow-Through
Phase**

___ "Riding a bicycle" smoothly

Step 6 Back Crawl Kicking

Propulsion is a significant function of the swimming kick. There are several different kicking motions used for propulsion: the crawl kick, the back crawl kick, the scissors kick, the breaststroke kick, and the dolphin kick. You should continue to learn them all in advanced swimming courses.

Because it resembles the forward-backward motion of the legs during walking, the easiest kick to learn for propulsion in a back float position is the back crawl kick. (You will also learn the crawl kick and a version of the breaststroke kick later in this book. If your legs are so heavy that they do not come to the surface during sculling or stroking, and if you have learned the support kick in Step 5 out of necessity, you may wish to learn the propulsive kick while wearing a support belt.)

WHY IS THE BACK CRAWL KICK IMPORTANT?

The back crawl kick is the first propulsive movement of the legs you will learn. It should not be considered a *necessary* motion in swimming but, rather, an optional motion to aid your arms in moving your body. There is a natural tendency to move the legs while swimming. Though they may not be needed for supporting movements, it is still important to move them in an efficient manner to provide

propulsion, rather than to allow them to cause resistance by dragging.

Remember, though, that the back crawl kick is not the primary propulsive force for the backstroke. It can be tiring, because it uses a considerable amount of energy for the propulsion it produces. Use it sparingly at this stage in your learning.

HOW TO DO THE BACK CRAWL KICK

Start from a back float position. Scull or stroke to bring your feet up near the surface. Your ankles must be *totally* relaxed. Drop one leg downward about 24 to 30 inches; keep its knee straight. Water pressure forces your relaxed, loose ankle to hook during this downward motion. Allow your knee to bend slightly as you begin to move your leg upward again. This upward movement presses your foot into a pointed-toe position. Move your leg upward until its knee is just under the surface. Stop your knee at this point and straighten your leg. With your foot, ''spoon'' the water upward and backward, raising a ''mound'' of water. Move your other leg in the same manner, but in the opposite direction, causing an alternating upward and backward thrust of the feet against the water. If your ankles are truly relaxed, your toes naturally turn inward somewhat (see Figure 6.1).

Figure 6.1 Keys to Success: Back Crawl Kicking

**Preparation
Phase**

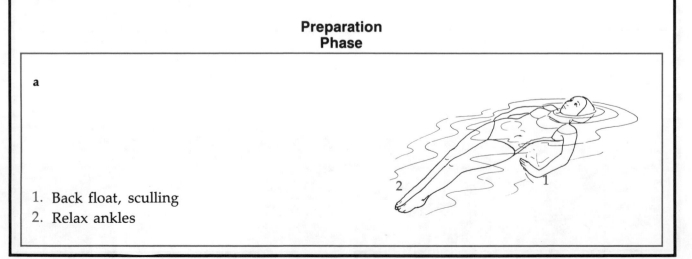

a

1. Back float, sculling
2. Relax ankles

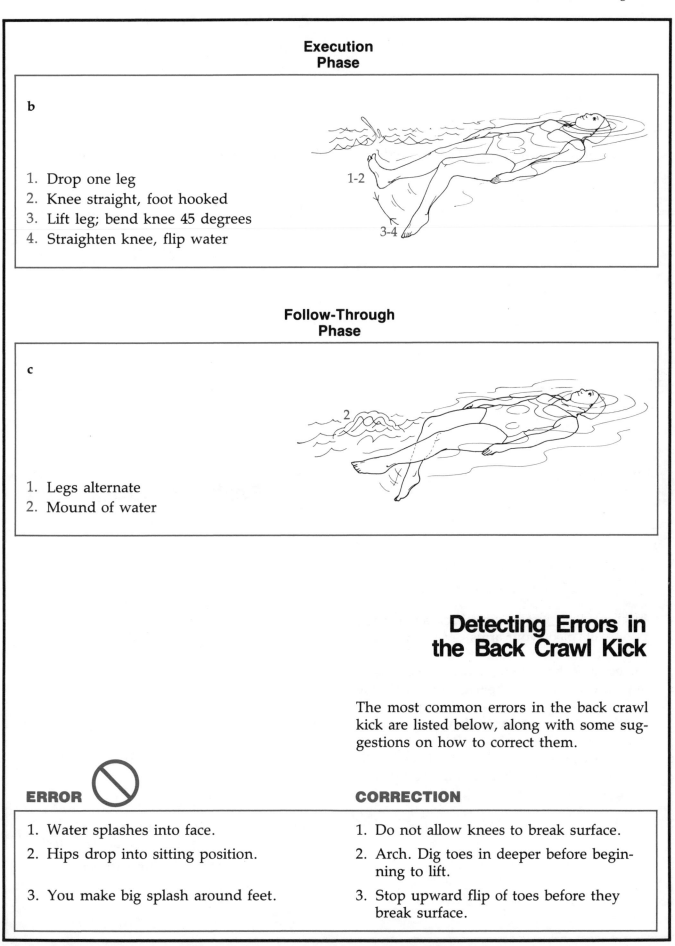

**Execution
Phase**

b

1. Drop one leg
2. Knee straight, foot hooked
3. Lift leg; bend knee 45 degrees
4. Straighten knee, flip water

1-2

3-4

**Follow-Through
Phase**

c

1. Legs alternate
2. Mound of water

2

Detecting Errors in the Back Crawl Kick

The most common errors in the back crawl kick are listed below, along with some suggestions on how to correct them.

ERROR

CORRECTION

ERROR	CORRECTION
1. Water splashes into face.	1. Do not allow knees to break surface.
2. Hips drop into sitting position.	2. Arch. Dig toes in deeper before beginning to lift.
3. You make big splash around feet.	3. Stop upward flip of toes before they break surface.

ERROR 🚫	CORRECTION
4. No (or little) propulsion is produced.	4. Relax ankle, allow foot to turn inward on up-thrust. Do not allow knee to bend more than 60 degrees on up-thrust.

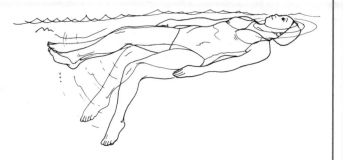

Back Crawl Kick Drills

1. Wide-Arm Bracket Drill for Back Crawl Kick

In chest-deep water, your back against the pool wall, place your arms out to the sides, your elbows on the edge of the pool. Grasp the edge of the pool with your hands, bend at your waist, and do the back crawl kick. Try to flip water up and back with the toes as if to splash someone standing beyond your feet. Allow your ankles to be flexible and floppy. Press downward with one leg to offset the lifting motion of the other. Count the upward thrusts of each foot.

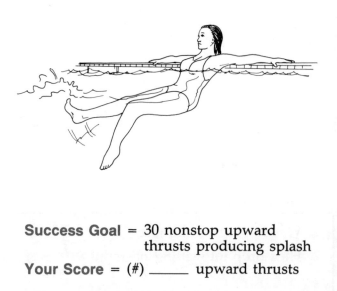

Success Goal = 30 nonstop upward thrusts producing splash

Your Score = (#) _____ upward thrusts

2. *Tight Bracket Drill for Back Crawl Kick*

Stand as above, except reach back over your shoulders to grasp the wall, your elbows in front of your face and your forearms close to either side of your head. Keep your shoulders underwater. Keep your body straight. Make a mound of water above your feet without actually splashing. Count the upward thrusts in which turbulence results without splashing.

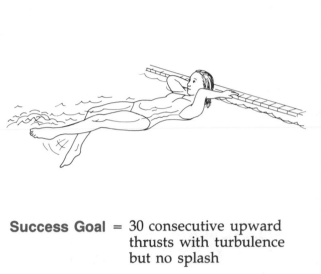

Success Goal = 30 consecutive upward thrusts with turbulence but no splash

Your Score = (#) _____ consecutive thrusts without splash

3. *Kickboard Drill for Back Crawl Kick*

In shallow water, hold a kickboard against your chest. Lie back into a back float position. Lift your chin slightly. Kick upward and backward as above with minimal splashing and minimal bend at hips. Emphasize the backward thrust. Move headfirst through the water for distance.

Success Goal = pool width or 45 feet

Your Score = (#) _____ feet

4. *Deep-Water Kickboard Drill for Back Crawl Kick*

With your instructor watching, start in a back float position at the deep end of the pool with a kickboard held against your chest. Kick to the shallow end of the pool.

Success Goal = one pool length or 75 feet

Your Score = (#) _____ feet

5. Deep-Water Back Crawl Kick Drill With Sculling

In deep water, with your instructor watching, begin a back float with sculling. Add the kick. Keep your hips near the surface.

Success Goal = one pool length or 75 feet

Your Score = (#) _____ feet

6. Deep-Water Back Crawl Kick Drill With Pulling

In deep water, with your instructor watching, start a back float with stroking. Add the kick. Keep kicking easily while your arms rest in the gliding position. Lie back. Keep your hips up.

Success Goal = one pool length or 75 feet

Your Score = (#) _____ feet

7. Deep-Water Back Crawl Kick Drill With Turn

Starting in shallow water, with your instructor watching, pull and kick into deep water. Continue to kick, but stop pulling with one arm. Using only the other arm, turn until you are heading back into shallow water. Then pull with both arms until you return to shallow water.

Success Goal = 5 deep-water turns in each direction

Your Score = (#) _____ deep-water turns

If you have been wearing a support belt for this step, go into shallow water and try Drills 5, 6, and 7 without the belt. You may find that you no longer need the support. If you are confident that you no longer need the belt, try the drills in deep water with your instructor watching.

Back Crawl Kick
Keys to Success Checklist

A mound of water at your feet indicates that you have attained the ability to do a crawl stroke kick, but the consistency and variations in that mound are qualitative items that only a trained instructor can evaluate. Ask your teacher or another knowledgeable person to evaluate your kick qualitatively, using the checklist below to indicate areas in which you could improve.

**Preparation
Phase**

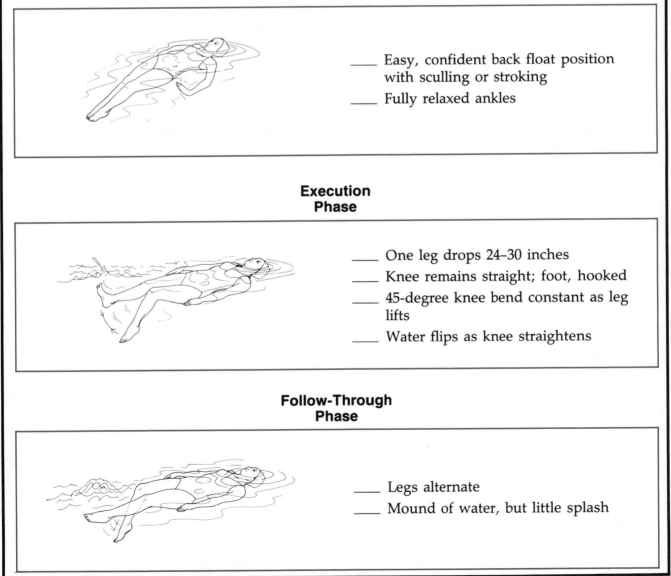

____ Easy, confident back float position with sculling or stroking

____ Fully relaxed ankles

**Execution
Phase**

____ One leg drops 24–30 inches

____ Knee remains straight; foot, hooked

____ 45-degree knee bend constant as leg lifts

____ Water flips as knee straightens

**Follow-Through
Phase**

____ Legs alternate

____ Mound of water, but little splash

Step 7 Prone Float

Swimming on your back can be learned quickly and easily and can save you from drowning, but there are many advantages to being able to swim in a prone position as well. Some of the most efficient stroke patterns, such as the crawl and breaststroke, are performed in the prone position. The main disadvantage to prone swimming is the increased importance of breath control—probably the most difficult skill in swimming. You will learn more about breath control in this step.

Those who are nonbuoyant and have been wearing a float belt for support in the previous steps may need to use the support belt again, because no supporting motions are used in this step. The belt should be worn at waist level.

WHY IS THE PRONE FLOAT IMPORTANT?

The prone float is the basis for all the prone swimming strokes. Once again, remember that *all* swimming is nothing more than pulling yourself through the water while floating.

Your natural buoyancy and the air in your lungs keep you afloat. The position in which you float is determined by balancing yourself around the center of buoyancy in your lungs.

HOW TO DO A PRONE FLOAT

To do a prone float, stand in chest-deep water with your hands at your sides. Take a deep breath and bend forward. Lower your face into the water until your ears are covered. Allow your fingertips to slide down your thighs to your shins. As your hands reach your knees, let your feet rise from the bottom. You should be floating with your arms and legs hanging down like the tentacles of a jellyfish. Hold your breath while you fully extend your arms forward and your legs backward. Hold this position only momentarily before bringing your hands down and bending at the waist again to put your hands on your knees. Immediately slide your hands up your thighs as you place your feet on the pool bottom and stand (see Figure 7.1). Exhale.

Figure 7.1 Keys to Success: Prone Float

Preparation Phase

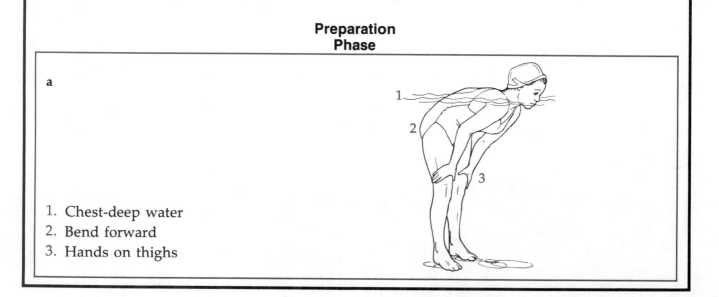

a

1. Chest-deep water
2. Bend forward
3. Hands on thighs

**Execution
Phase**

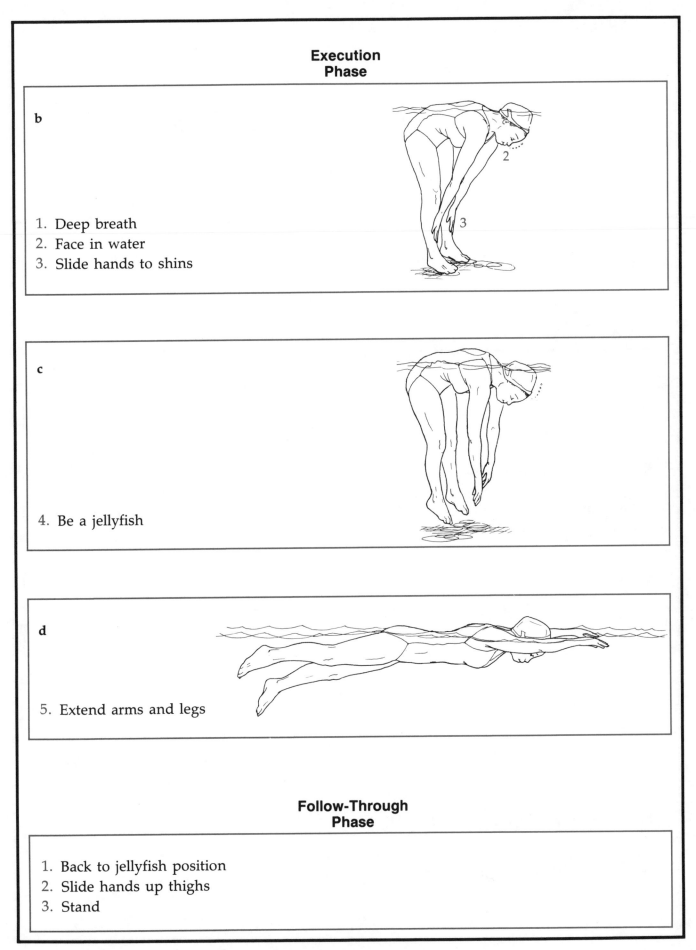

b

1. Deep breath
2. Face in water
3. Slide hands to shins

c

4. Be a jellyfish

d

5. Extend arms and legs

**Follow-Through
Phase**

1. Back to jellyfish position
2. Slide hands up thighs
3. Stand

Detecting Errors in the Prone Float

Learning to do a prone float is easier if you can compare correct and incorrect techniques. The most common errors in doing the prone float are listed below, along with some suggestions on how to correct them.

ERROR

CORRECTION

1. Nose fills with water.

2. Body sinks; feet remain on bottom.

3. You have trouble standing again.

4. You roll to side while in the extended position.

1. Lift chin slightly, blow one small bubble through nose.

2. Take a bigger breath; avoid exhaling. (Those who needed float belts for back float will also need them now.)

3. Hold jellyfish position with hands on knees until steady, then stand.

4. Do not arch back; spread arms and legs slightly apart.

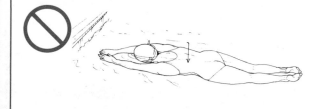

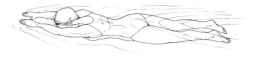

Prone Floating Drills

1. Jellyfish Prone Float

Repeat the process described in Figure 7.1, increasing the time in the extended prone float position. Count seconds.

Success Goal = 10 seconds floating

Your Score = (#) _____ seconds

2. Prone Float With Kickboard From Bottom

In chest-deep water, hold a kickboard at arm's length with both hands. Take a deep breath, put face in water, and push off bottom into extended prone float position. While floating, *lift* on kickboard to keep your feet up. When ready to stand, press on the kickboard and bring your feet under you before standing. Count seconds.

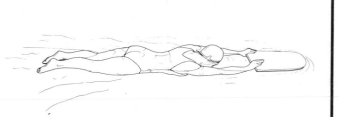

Success Goal = 20 seconds floating

Your Score = (#) _____ seconds

3. Prone Float With Kickboard From Wall

In chest-deep water, stand with your back to the wall, holding a kickboard at arm's length. Place one foot against wall, take a deep breath, place your face in the water, and shove off with your back foot. Extend into a prone float and glide until motion ceases. Streamline your body, especially your toes. If your feet sink, *lift* on the board, your feet will rise. *Press* on board to stand.

Success Goal = 15 feet gliding

Your Score = (#) _____ feet gliding

4. Prone Float to the Wall

In chest-deep water, stand facing the wall, about 6 feet away. Do not hold a kickboard. Extend your arms forward, place your face in the water, and jump forward from the bottom. Hold a prone float position until your fingers touch the wall. Press on the wall to stand. Repeat, each time a little farther from the wall. If you do not reach the wall, press on the water to stand.

Success Goal = 12 feet gliding to wall

Your Score = (#) _____ feet gliding

5. *Prone Float From Wall*

In chest-deep water, stand with your back to the wall, one foot against wall behind you. Extend your arms forward (no kickboard), take a breath, put your face in the water, and push off the wall. Streamline your body. Glide for distance. When forward motion ceases, press downward with both arms and hands while drawing your feet and knees up under you. Wait until your feet are under you before you attempt to stand.

Success Goal = 20 feet gliding

Your Score = (#) _____ feet gliding

Prone Floating
Keys to Success Checklist

A float is a float is a float—right? Not necessarily! Success Goals have been based on quantitative measures. However, it is also important to measure how well you have attained those quantitative goals. Ask an expert to evaluate your prone float qualitatively. Is it tense? Do you make it look hard? Does your apprehension show? Let an expert use the checklist below to identify areas in which you could improve the quality of your skills.

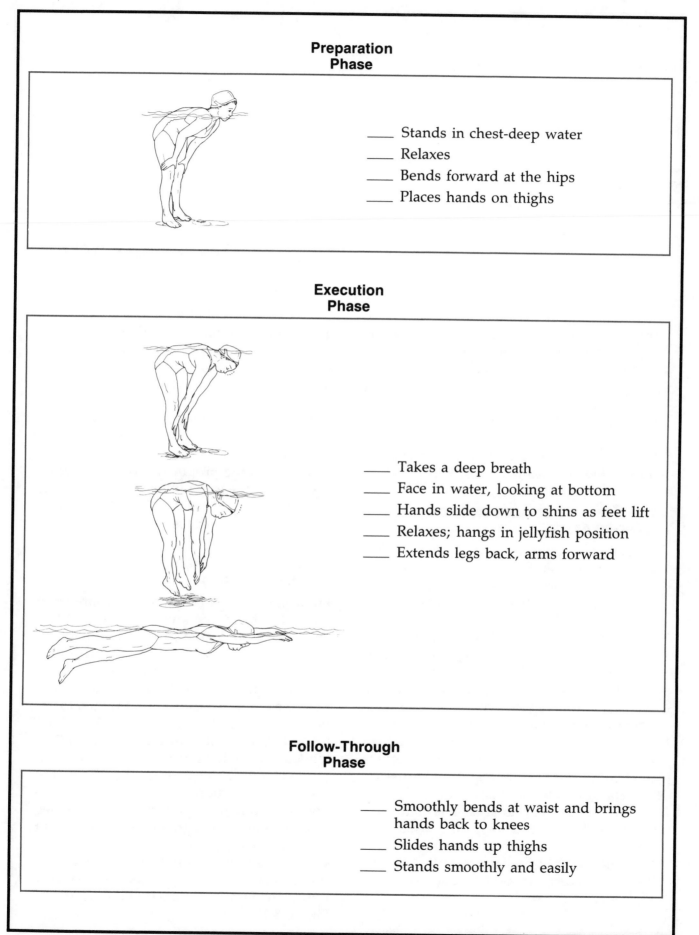

**Preparation
Phase**

____ Stands in chest-deep water

____ Relaxes

____ Bends forward at the hips

____ Places hands on thighs

**Execution
Phase**

____ Takes a deep breath

____ Face in water, looking at bottom

____ Hands slide down to shins as feet lift

____ Relaxes; hangs in jellyfish position

____ Extends legs back, arms forward

**Follow-Through
Phase**

____ Smoothly bends at waist and brings
hands back to knees

____ Slides hands up thighs

____ Stands smoothly and easily

Step 8 Beginner Kick

We mentioned in Step 5 that kicking serves three important functions: balance, support, and propulsion. The beginner kick in the prone float position performs all three. Primarily, it provides support for your feet and legs while you begin to learn arm strokes in the prone position. In so doing, it also provides minimal propulsion, and counterbalances the pull of each arm, keeping the torso relatively steady.

WHY IS THE BEGINNER KICK IMPORTANT?

Actually the kick is of little importance, but it must be utilized because of human nature. For one thing, beginners invariably and inherently believe that they must press down on the water to stay at the surface. You have proven to yourself that it is not necessary to do so. Yet, when you begin to make propulsive movements with your arms, you almost certainly press downward somewhat, despite the best efforts to teach you otherwise. This downward pressure causes your feet and legs to sink rapidly in the prone position. You then need some kicking motion to counteract this downward push of the hands and arms.

Second, it is human nature to move your legs when moving your arms; it is quite difficult to hold your legs still especially while your arms are making very large movements. Such movement of the legs, if not correctly directed, can be a major source of drag, decreasing the efficiency of the stroke.

So, although the kick is not really needed and should be minimized, it is very important that you learn it. It will reduce the drag of your legs, because you cannot hold them still. It will help keep them from sinking, because you *will* push down on the water. Furthermore, it will, just incidentally, provide *some* forward propulsive force. You will learn very quickly, however, that the price you pay in effort is not really worth the propulsive force produced. If you learn the arm pull in Step 9 correctly, you can save a lot of effort by using the kick only to provide balance.

HOW TO PERFORM THE BEGINNER KICK

From a prone float position with your face in the water, bend one knee, raising your foot and calf to a 90-degree angle behind you. Immediately kick your foot and calf downward again while raising your other foot and calf 90 degrees. Kick alternately, first one leg and then the other. A flexible ankle is vital to letting your foot be naturally hooked (toes toward knee) on its upward motion and extended on its downward motion. Your extended foot has greater thrust in the downward direction, providing upward support. In addition, as your foot and lower leg extend from a 90-degree bend to a straight position, there is a backward force that provides some forward propulsion. As you kick, try to make the kick progressively smaller until your feet stay mostly underwater (see Figure 8.1).

Figure 8.1   Keys to Success: *Beginner Kick*

Preparation Phase

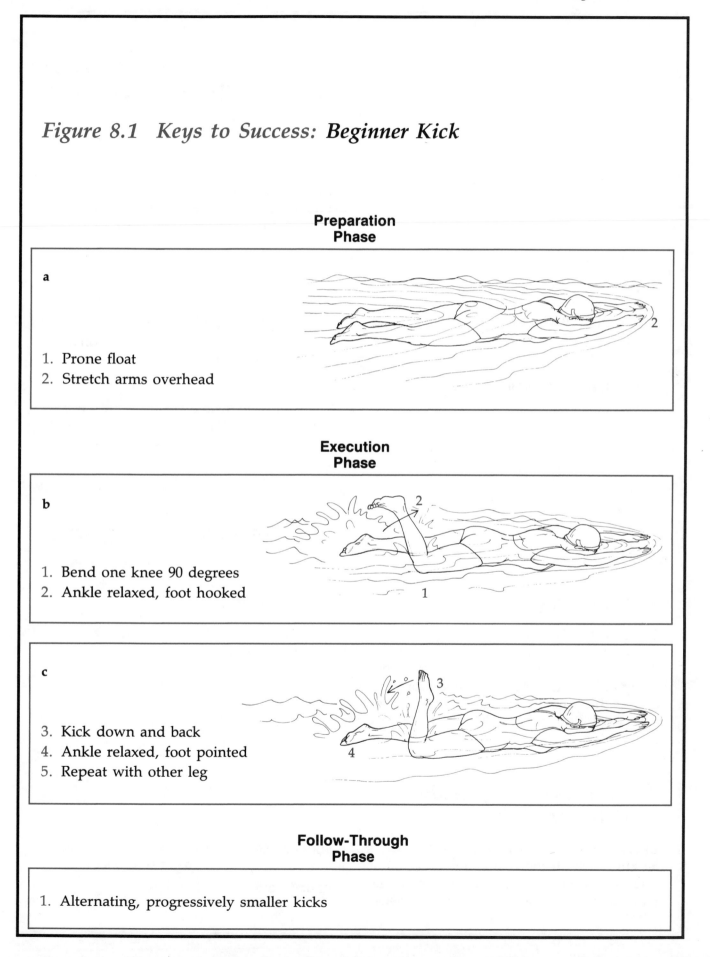

a

1. Prone float
2. Stretch arms overhead

Execution Phase

b

1. Bend one knee 90 degrees
2. Ankle relaxed, foot hooked

c

3. Kick down and back
4. Ankle relaxed, foot pointed
5. Repeat with other leg

Follow-Through Phase

1. Alternating, progressively smaller kicks

Detecting Errors in the Beginner Kick

Learning to recognize a well-executed beginner kick is easier if you are aware of some of the most common technique faults. The most common beginner kick errors are listed below, along with suggestions on how to correct them.

ERROR 🚫	CORRECTION
1. You make no forward progress.	1. Bend your knee, kick back.
2. Feet sink.	2. Flex ankle, making foot hooked on up movement and pointed on down.
3. You make big splashes.	3. Narrow the kick, raise chin.
4. You move backward.	4. Result of inflexible ankles; bend knee more to compensate.

Beginner Kicking Drills

1. Float and Beginner Kick

The downward and backward forces are about equal in this kick. Because it is hard to measure the support force, you can measure efficiency easily only by the distance moved forward, though this is not the primary function of the kick. Repeat the process described in Figure 8.1 and try for distance on one breath.

Success Goal = 20 feet on one breath

Your Score = (#) _____ feet

2. Kickboard Glide and Beginner Kick

In shallow water, hold a kickboard at arm's length. Push off the wall and glide as far as you can on one breath. Then turn back and kick for the same distance. Which is easier?

Success Goal = realization that gliding is easier than kicking

Your Score = _____ is easier

3. Beginner Kick and Breathing With Kickboard

In shallow water, hold a kickboard at arm's length, push off the side of the pool, and kick across the pool. When you need a breath, press on the kickboard, thrust your chin forward, and breathe. Avoid *lifting* your head; keep your chin at water level. Then drop your face into the water and *lift* on the board until you need another breath.

Success Goal = one pool width or 45 feet

Your Score = (#) _____ feet

4. Beginner Kick and Breathing Without Kickboard

In shallow water, push off the side of the pool in prone float position and begin kicking. When you need a breath, press down with your hands and arms as you thrust your chin forward long enough to get a quick breath. Avoid lifting your head; keep your chin at water level. Exhale and inhale quickly through your mouth.

Success Goal = 3 successful breaths

Your Score = (#) _____ successful breaths

5. Beginner Kick and Breathing, Head Up

Hold a kickboard at arm's length. Push off the wall in prone float position, but hold your chin at water level so you can breathe whenever you wish. Notice the tendency for your feet to sink. The harder you press on the board or the higher you raise your head, the more your feet tend to sink.

Success Goal = one pool width or 45 feet with head up

Your Score = (#) _____ feet with head up

6. Beginner Kick and Breathing With Chin on Board

Put both arms along the length of a kickboard in front of you. Adjust the board so that your chin rests on it in prone float position. Push off the side of the pool in shallow water and kick across the pool. Keep your chin on the board, so you can breathe when you wish.

Success Goal = one pool width or 45 feet

Your Score = (#) _____ feet

7. Beginner Kick for Extra Support

In neck-deep water, hold onto the side of the pool and kick. As you kick, press on the side of the pool until your head and neck are above water (water at shoulder level). Note how your feet sink. Kick harder to keep them up while holding head and neck out of the water. See how long you can maintain this position.

Success Goal = 30 seconds

Your Score = (#) _____ seconds

8. Beginner Kick Evaluation Drill

Press very hard on a kickboard while kicking in the prone position. Try to raise your head and shoulders high, still keeping your feet at the surface. Then hold the board at arm's length and put your face in the water as you kick. Compare the amount of energy needed each way.

Draw conclusions about whether a kick is an efficient way to keep your head out of the water, and whether it is profitable in terms of energy consumption to press downward on the water when swimming.

Success Goal = realization that pressing downward on water consumes a lot of energy for minimal results

Your Score = _____ the extent to which you realize this

Beginner Kick
Keys to Success Checklist

You have been testing yourself quantitatively by attaining each of the Step 8 Success Goals. Fluidity and efficiency are qualitative aspects that are also important. Ask your teacher, coach, or a trained observer to evaluate your beginner kick qualitatively according to the checklist below. He or she may decide to create an individual practice program for you.

Preparation Phase

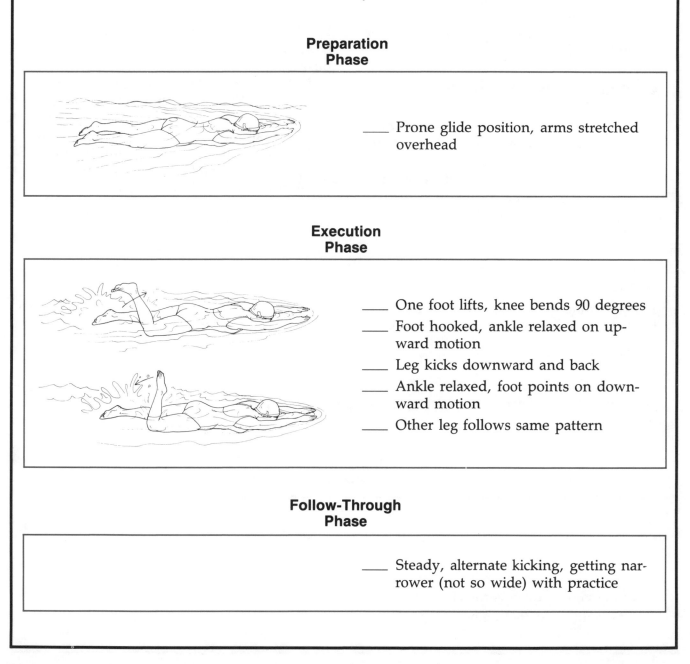

_____ Prone glide position, arms stretched overhead

Execution Phase

_____ One foot lifts, knee bends 90 degrees

_____ Foot hooked, ankle relaxed on upward motion

_____ Leg kicks downward and back

_____ Ankle relaxed, foot points on downward motion

_____ Other leg follows same pattern

Follow-Through Phase

_____ Steady, alternate kicking, getting narrower (not so wide) with practice

Step 9 **Beginner Pull**

You are now able to float and glide in a face-down position. To continue forward movement in this position, you must apply force against the water in a backward direction. The easiest method for exerting a backward force on the water is to press backward with your hands and arms. The beginner pull is not efficient enough to be packaged into a "name" stroke, but it does have the advantage of providing propulsion without affecting your stable floating body position.

WHY IS THE BEGINNER PULL IMPORTANT?

The beginner pull is a transition arm stroke. It allows you to move forward through the water while you learn to breathe in a prone position. Attempting the more efficient crawl arm stroke at this point would cause disruption of your body position and result in your swallowing a lot of water.

HOW TO EXECUTE THE BEGINNER PULL

From a prone glide position, your arms extended forward, flex your right wrist so your fingers point down, your palm facing back. Begin the pull with your forearm and hand, keeping your elbow high. Bend your elbow so your hand and forearm move inward and backward. Straighten your wrist as your forearm moves. Your hand should now be in the centerline of your body, directly under your nose; your elbow should be bent 90 degrees, and your wrist should be straight. With your hand, push water directly back under your body about 6 inches from your chest. As you push past your waist, straighten your elbow and allow your hand to move outward to your right thigh. When your thumb touches your thigh, begin the recovery by keeping your elbow close as you draw your hand along your body to your chin. Then turn your palm down and push your hand forward, fingers leading, to full arm extension. Pause. Transfer your attention to your left arm. Repeat these motions with your left arm (see Figure 9.1).

Figure 9.1 *Keys to Success:* **Beginner Pull**

Preparation Phase

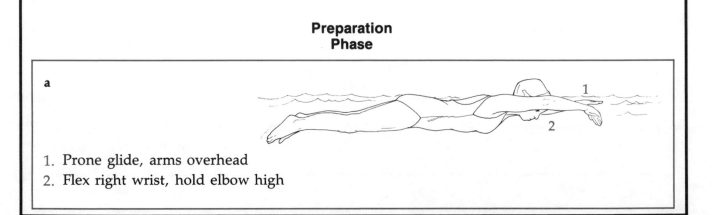

1. Prone glide, arms overhead
2. Flex right wrist, hold elbow high

Execution
Phase

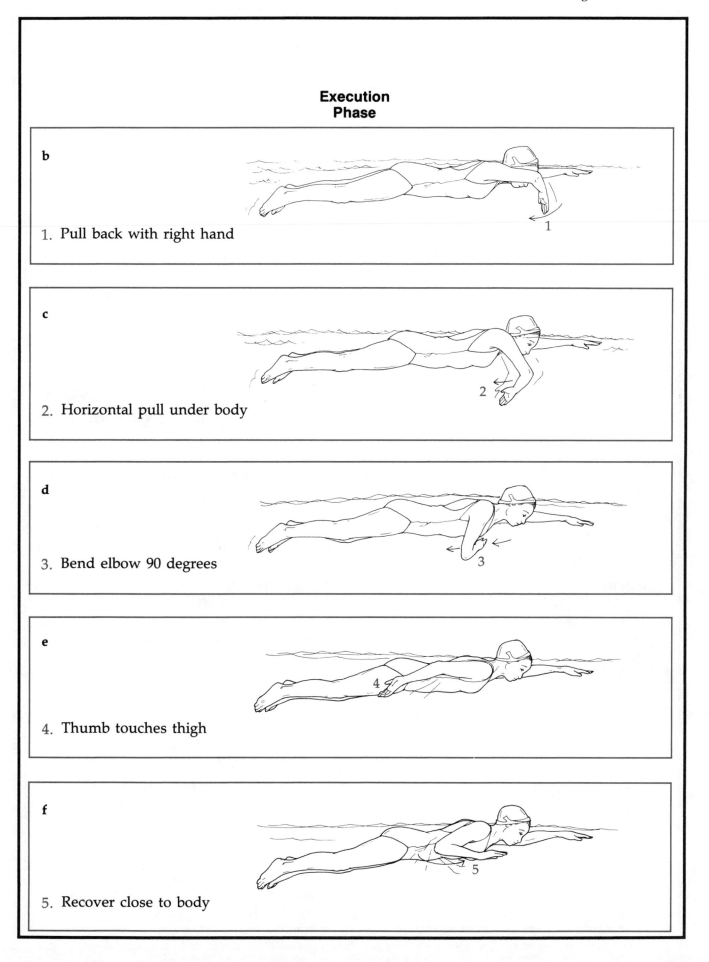

b

1. Pull back with right hand

c

2. Horizontal pull under body

d

3. Bend elbow 90 degrees

e

4. Thumb touches thigh

f

5. Recover close to body

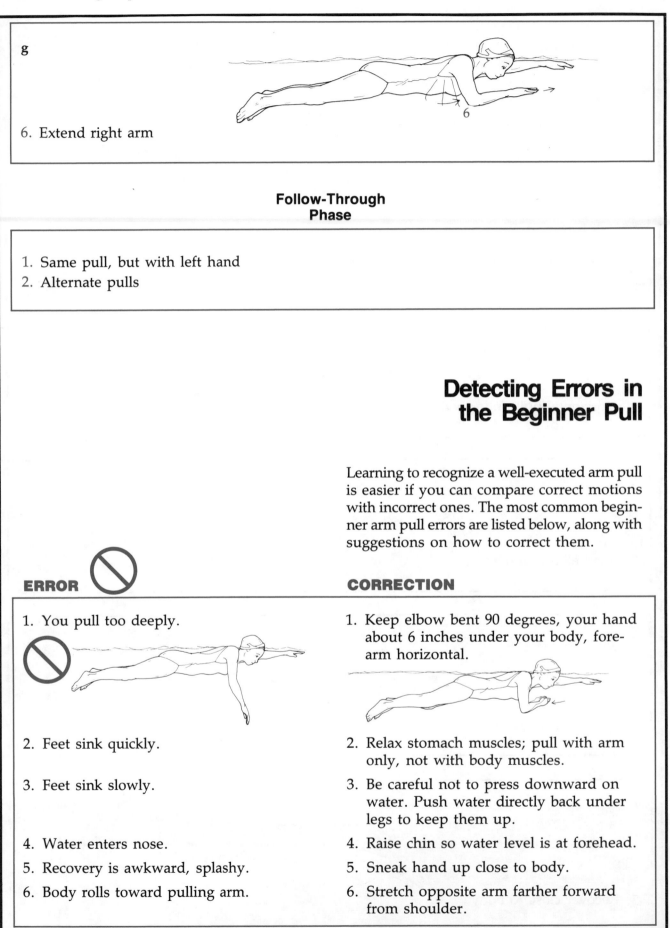

g

6. Extend right arm

**Follow-Through
Phase**

1. Same pull, but with left hand
2. Alternate pulls

Detecting Errors in the Beginner Pull

Learning to recognize a well-executed arm pull is easier if you can compare correct motions with incorrect ones. The most common beginner arm pull errors are listed below, along with suggestions on how to correct them.

ERROR | **CORRECTION**

1. You pull too deeply.

1. Keep elbow bent 90 degrees, your hand about 6 inches under your body, forearm horizontal.

2. Feet sink quickly.

2. Relax stomach muscles; pull with arm only, not with body muscles.

3. Feet sink slowly.

3. Be careful not to press downward on water. Push water directly back under legs to keep them up.

4. Water enters nose.

4. Raise chin so water level is at forehead.

5. Recovery is awkward, splashy.

5. Sneak hand up close to body.

6. Body rolls toward pulling arm.

6. Stretch opposite arm farther forward from shoulder.

Beginner Pulling Drills

1. Glide and Beginner Pull

Do a prone glide with a push-off from the wall. Begin stroking when glide slows. Concentrate on full-length pulling. Try for distance on 2 strokes. Keep your face down and hold your breath. Do not even think about your feet; let them do whatever they want to do.

Success Goal = 6 feet beyond your best glide distance

Your Score = (#) _____ feet beyond glide

2. Beginner Pulls per Breath

Push off the wall in a prone glide. See how many *full* strokes you can make on one breath. Do not hurry the strokes. Do not kick; keep your feet together.

Success Goal = 6 strokes

Your Score = (#) _____ strokes

3. Beginner Pulls With Leg Float

Hold a kickboard or a pull-buoy (leg float) between your knees when you push off from the wall. Try to increase your pulling distance on one breath. Release the board or float before trying to stand. Make each pull full-length.

Success Goal = one pool width or 45 feet

Your Score = (#) _____ feet

4. Beginner Pull With Mask, Snorkel

Ask your instructor to fit you with a mask and snorkel and to explain their use. When you are comfortable breathing through the snorkel, use it while pulling. Regulate your breathing so that you are inhaling while you pull

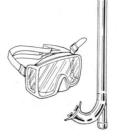

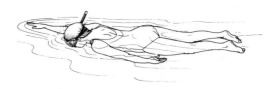

with one arm, and exhaling while you pull with your other arm. Keep face down. Do not kick; keep feet together.

Success Goal = one pool width or 45 feet while breathing correctly

Your Score = (#) _____ feet while breathing correctly

5. Turning With Beginner Pulls, Mask, Snorkel, Leg Float

Hold a kickboard or pull-buoy between your knees, use a mask and snorkel, and practice the beginner pull. Be sure each pull is full-length. After 4 pulls, look and reach to the left as you continue pulling. You should be able to turn to the left. Then look and reach to the right as you pull. Turn to the right.

Success Goal = alternating 4 left and 4 right 90-degree turns without stopping

Your Score = (#) _____ alternating left and right turns

6. Beginner Pulls and Turns With Mask, Snorkel

Repeat Drill 5 without a leg support. Allow your legs to kick if it seems more comfortable. If they sink, correct your pull so there is no downward force. All the push should be in a backward direction, parallel to the surface.

Success Goal = alternating 4 left and 4 right 90-degree turns without stopping while keeping legs near surface

Your Score = (#) _____ alternating left and right turns, legs near surface

7. Deep Water Turns, Beginner Pull, Mask, Snorkel, Floats

With your instructor watching, use mask, snorkel, and leg support. Pull from shallow water into deep water, do a wide turn, and return to shallow water.

Success Goal = 4 round trips with rests between

Your Score = (#) _____ round trips with rests between

Beginner Pull
Keys to Success Checklist

A qualitative evaluation of the beginner pull includes assessing your ease of movement, length of pull, actual forward progress achieved, and apparent confidence. Have your teacher or a trained observer check for these and each of the other items below. This will help determine which aspects need additional drills or other training attention to improve your overall beginner pulling quality.

Preparation Phase

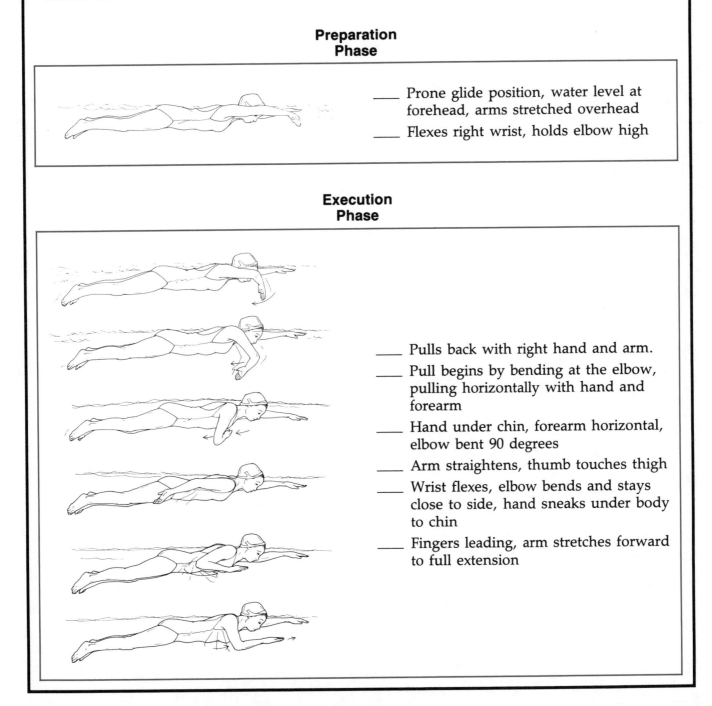

____ Prone glide position, water level at forehead, arms stretched overhead

____ Flexes right wrist, holds elbow high

Execution Phase

____ Pulls back with right hand and arm.

____ Pull begins by bending at the elbow, pulling horizontally with hand and forearm

____ Hand under chin, forearm horizontal, elbow bent 90 degrees

____ Arm straightens, thumb touches thigh

____ Wrist flexes, elbow bends and stays close to side, hand sneaks under body to chin

____ Fingers leading, arm stretches forward to full extension

**Follow-Through
Phase**

____ Other arm follows same pattern
____ Alternate, rhythmical pulls

Step 10 **Breathing**

Breath control during swimming begins with controlling your breath for buoyancy (in Step 1) and for prolonging your float (in Step 2 and in all subsequent steps). This step will concentrate on integration of breath control with prone swimming techniques.

WHY IS BREATHING IMPORTANT?

Why indeed? Of course we must breathe, but we have considerable leeway in *how* we breathe. Control of your breathing to make it fit your swimming stroke pattern is probably the most difficult, but the most rewarding, skill required in the sport of swimming. You must practice it until it becomes habitual. When you have become truly proficient, you will probably find yourself practicing swimming breathing patterns involuntarily every time you step into a shower! Correct breathing patterns differentiate the polished, expert swimmer from the novice. *Breath control habits are vital to swimming.*

ABOUT BREATHING

In swimming, you cannot always breathe when you want to—you must breathe when you can. Often the time allowed for breathing in the rhythm of a stroke is very short. Your nose is not large enough to allow you to take in the amount of air you require in the time allowed. This problem is solved by breathing through your mouth. Exhaling through your nose is important because it helps to keep the water out, but the volume

of air you must exhale in the time allowed requires that you exhale partly through your mouth as well.

Your buoyancy depends upon the amount of air in your lungs. You cannot hold a full breath while swimming, but you can keep your lungs more nearly completely inflated by inhaling fully and exhaling about half the air on each breath. Thus you can "breathe off the top of your lungs." If this results in breathlessness, you must revert to full and complete exhalations and inhalations to meet your body's oxygen demand.

The drills in this step will lead you through a progression to establish proper breathing techniques gradually.

HOW TO CONTROL YOUR BREATHING WHILE SWIMMING

Always inhale only through your mouth. Exhale at least partly through your nose. Start by lying prone in the water. Hold onto the edge of the pool with both hands, with a float between your knees. Take a breath through your mouth and place your face in the water, looking slightly forward so the waterline is on your forehead. Exhale fully through your nose. The air comes out easier if you "hum" it out, using your voice. When a full exhalation has been made, tilt your head back until your chin is just at water level. Do not *lift* your head; only *tilt* it by thrusting the chin forward. Open your mouth wide to inhale quickly, then drop your face into the water again to exhale (see Figure 10.1).

*Figure 10.1 Keys to Success: **Breathing***

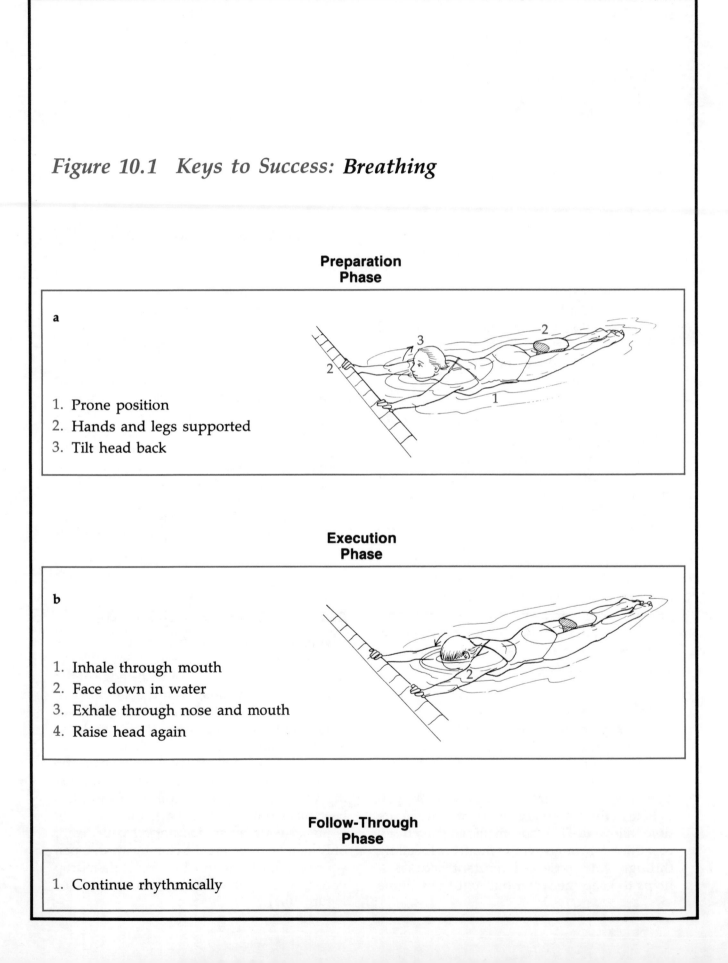

**Preparation
Phase**

a

1. Prone position
2. Hands and legs supported
3. Tilt head back

**Execution
Phase**

b

1. Inhale through mouth
2. Face down in water
3. Exhale through nose and mouth
4. Raise head again

**Follow-Through
Phase**

1. Continue rhythmically

Detecting Breathing Errors

Learning to recognize good breathing habits is easier if you can compare good and bad practices. The most common breathing errors are listed below, along with some suggestions for correcting them.

ERROR 🚫

CORRECTION

ERROR	CORRECTION
1. Water enters nose when face is down.	1. Keep waterline at forehead. Exhale partly through nose.
2. Head and shoulders rise above water during inhalation.	2. Tilt head instead of lifting; keep chin at water level.
3. Difficulty in exhaling exists.	3. Use voice to hum.
4. Feet have a tendency to sink.	4. Put less pressure on hands. Keep head lower.
5. Breathlessness occurs when repeating.	5. Exhale fully, inhale deeply.

Breathing Drills

1. Bracket Drill, Breathing Forward

Practice the technique described in Figure 10.1 until you feel confident in getting each new breath.

Success Goal = 10 consecutive breaths

Your Score = (#) _____ consecutive breaths

2. Forward Breathing With Kickboard

Hold a kickboard with your fingertips at arm's length in front of you. With your face down, kick your legs and begin breathing as above. Try to put less and less pressure on the board when you breathe.

Success Goal = 10 consecutive breaths

Your Score = (#) _____ consecutive breaths

3. Forward Breathing, No Support

Set aside the kickboard and repeat the drill above. Press gently on the water, making sculling motions with your hands when you tilt your head to breathe.

Success Goal = 10 consecutive breaths

Your Score = (#) _____ consecutive breaths

4. Bracket and Leg Float, Side Breathing

Hold onto the side of the pool with both hands. Use a leg float to support your legs. Turn your head to one side, lay your ear on the water, and keep your mouth at water level. Breathe with your mouth just above the water. If you have difficulty, do not lift your head, but leave your ear in the water and turn your head farther to get your mouth slightly higher.

Success Goal = 10 consecutive breaths

Your Score = (#) _____ consecutive breaths

5. Bracket and Leg Float, Rhythmic Side Breathing

Repeat Drill 4, but turn your face down to exhale and to the side to inhale. Leave your ear underwater when inhaling.

Success Goal = 10 consecutive breaths

Your Score = (#) _____ consecutive breaths

6. Rhythmic Side Breathing, Floating With Kickboard

Hold a kickboard at arm's length in front of you. Use a leg float. Do not try to move—just float motionless. Turn your head to one side, laying your ear on the water. Take a breath and turn your face downward to exhale. While you exhale, lift on the kickboard, to keep your feet up.

Success Goal = 10 consecutive breaths

Your Score = (#) _____ consecutive breaths

7. Rhythmic Side Breathing, Floating and Kicking

Hold a kickboard at arm's length while you float face downward. Kick your legs for support and breathe rhythmically to the side. Remove your breathing-side hand from the kickboard if it seems to be in the way, but replace it during exhalation.

Success Goal = 10 breaths

Your Score = (#) _____ breaths

8. Rhythmic Side Breathing for Distance

With a kickboard, kick while inhaling on the side and exhaling face downward. Do not count breaths but continue as long as you can breathe comfortably. Keep your ear on the water; do not lift your head—turn it.

Success Goal = one pool width or 45 feet

Your Score = (#) _____ feet

Breathing Keys to Success Checklist

You have been proving yourself quantitatively by attaining each of the Step 10 Success Goals. Qualitative evaluation of breathing skills, though, hinges on such intangibles as comfort and relaxation. Such things are difficult to measure, but if you ask your teacher or a trained observer to check the items listed below, the result will be a fair evaluation of the quality of your performance.

Preparation Phase

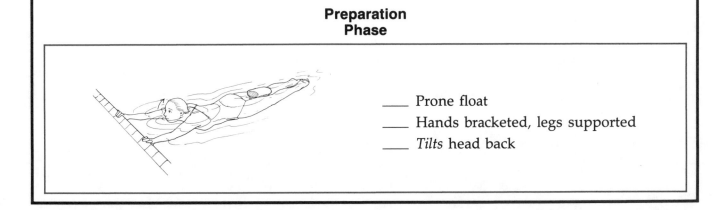

_____ Prone float

_____ Hands bracketed, legs supported

_____ *Tilts* head back

Execution
Phase

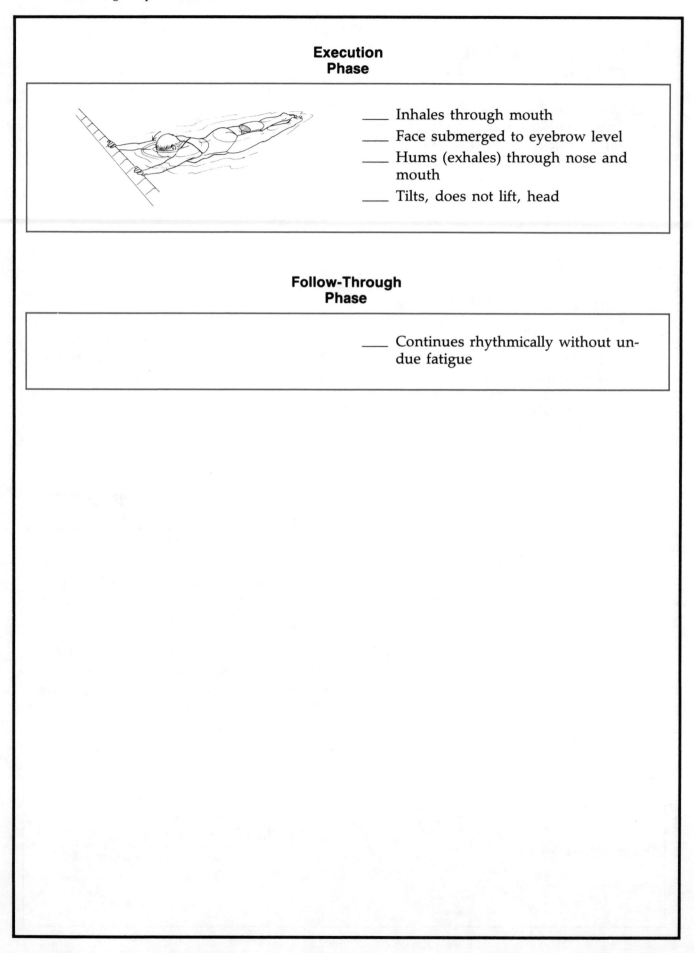

____ Inhales through mouth

____ Face submerged to eyebrow level

____ Hums (exhales) through nose and mouth

____ Tilts, does not lift, head

Follow-Through
Phase

____ Continues rhythmically without undue fatigue

Step 11   Pulling and Breathing

At this point you know how to pull and how to breathe. Combining the two skills (and possibly a third—kicking) requires a new element in breath control: timing. Until this point you were free to breathe at any time you felt the need. In this Step you will learn to make your breathing fit the timing of your stroke, rather than stroking to fit your breathing.

WHY IS THIS TWO-SKILL COMBINATION IMPORTANT?

The most efficient and fastest stroke known is the crawl. It is the essence of swimming, the stroke everyone visualizes when the word *swimming* is mentioned. You will not be an accomplished swimmer until you can do it well. You are on your way to learning it now, but it requires rhythmic breathing matched to your arm strokes. This two-skill combination is the point at which most novice swimmers stumble. If you follow the drill sequence in this step, though, you will breeze through the stumbling point with very little difficulty and be well on your way toward successful swimming.

HOW TO PULL AND BREATHE

Begin in a prone position, pull a stroke or two and exhale until the arm on your breathing side begins to pull. Start to turn your head up for a breath while your arm is making the first half of its pull. Your mouth should then be free to take a breath during the last half of the pull. Take a quick, but full, breath and return your face to the water as the breathing-side arm begins its recovery. Exhale during the pull and recovery of the non-breathing-side arm (see Figure 11.1).

Figure 11.1   Keys to Success: *Pulling and Breathing*

Preparation Phase

1. Prone position, pulling

Execution Phase

a

1. Exhale during non-breathing pull
2. Face down

1-2

b

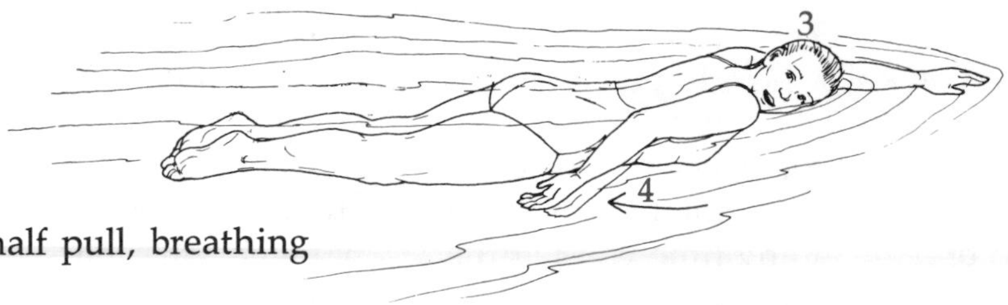

3. Roll face up, first half pull, breathing side
4. Breathe, second half pull breathing side

c

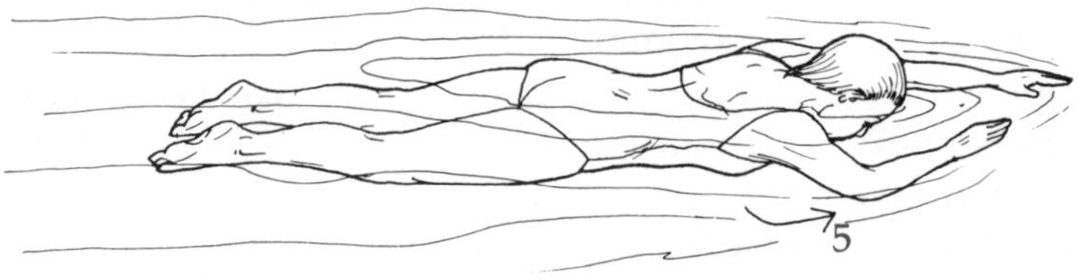

5. Face down, recovery breathing-side arm

Follow-Through Phase

1. Continue rhythmically

Detecting Errors in Pulling and Breathing

Learning to recognize good breathing technique is easier if you can compare good and bad practices. Some of the most common errors are listed below, along with some suggestions for correcting them.

ERROR 	CORRECTION
1. You breathe too early, arm interferes.	1. Turn your head but don't breathe during the first half of the pull.
2. You breathe too late, face rolls down.	2. Breathe during the last half of the pull.
3. You breathe water.	3. Roll face up farther. Use longer, slower pull.
4. Feet sink.	4. Roll, don't lift, head. Don't press down with hands.

Pulling and Breathing Drills

You have been completely free to breathe on whichever side feels most natural to you. You have probably chosen one side over the other without much conscious thought. These drills require you to inhale on the pull of the breathing-side arm and to exhale on the pull of the opposite arm—EVERY TIME! In this and many subsequent drills, you will be using the deep float leg support mentioned in the equipment list (see Figure 11.2).

Figure 11.2 Deep float leg support.

1. Pulling and Breathing With Deep Float, Mask, and Snorkel

Don mask and snorkel. With a deep leg float, do a prone float and beginner pull, but change the emphasis. Concentrate on timing your breathing to your stroke. Inhale *only* during the pull of the arm on your breathing side, and exhale *only* during the pull of the arm on the opposite side. Do not hold your breath at any time. Breathe on *every* ''breathing arm'' pull, and exhale on *every* opposite arm pull. Keep your face down all the time. Do not try to kick. Keep your feet close together.

Success Goal = 10 consecutive pulls with matched breathing

Your Score = (#) _____ consecutive pulls with matched breathing

2. *Pulling and Breathing With Deep Leg Support*

Attach a deep float to the ankle on your breathing side. In a floating position, keep your feet together and start by exhaling and pulling with the non-breathing-side arm. Then turn your head to your breathing side and inhale with the pull of your breathing-side arm. Leave your ear underwater. Turn your face back down to exhale while you pull with the opposite arm. Continue to pull and breathe.

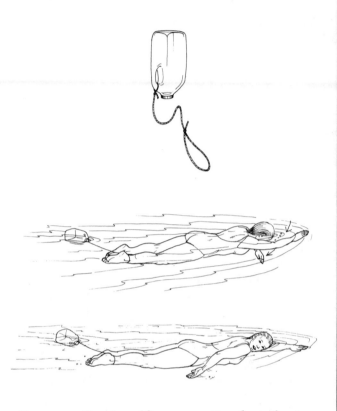

Success Goal = 10 consecutive breaths to the side while pulling

Your Score = (#) _____ breaths while pulling

3. *Timing Drill on Pulling and Breathing*

Repeat Drill 2, but with more emphasis on timing. Be sure to inhale while your breathing-side arm is *pulling*, not while it is recovering. The inhalation should be complete before the arm pull is completed. Allow your shoulders to roll as you turn to breathe, and to roll to the opposite side as you exhale. Continue across the pool.

Success Goal = one pool width or 45 feet

Your Score = (#) _____ feet

4. One-Arm Pull and Breathing With Kickboard

Hold a kickboard with both hands and use a deep float ankle float. Start by floating prone and exhaling, then hold the kickboard with the non-breathing hand as you pull and breathe on your breathing side. Replace your pulling hand on the board, and hold the float position while exhaling. Continue to pull only with the breathing-side arm while inhaling, and floating motionless while exhaling. To facilitate breathing, roll your shoulders while pulling. Keep your ear underwater.

Success Goal = 10 successful pulls and breaths

Your Score = (#) _____ pulls and breaths

5. Pulling and Breathing, No Support

Without a leg support float, allow your legs to move as they wish during pulling and breathing. Begin with an exhalation and a pull of the non-breathing arm. If your legs sink, be sure that your head is down during exhalation and that your ear is on the water during inhalation. Be sure to eliminate any downward push on the water with your hands. The pull must be horizontal under your body. Push the water backward under the centerline of your body.

Success Goal = one pool width or 45 feet

Your Score = (#) _____ feet

6. Pull, Kick, and Breathe, No Support

Start from a prone float position. Begin to kick. After 4 or 5 kicks, begin to pull and breathe to the side. Start with an exhalation and a pull of the non-breathing arm. Continue to kick while pulling and breathing. If you lose coordination, stop and start over. Keep the kick small; do not emphasize the kick. Breathe on *every* pull of the breathing-side arm.

Success Goal = one pool width or 45 feet

Your Score = (#) _____ feet

7. Shallow-Water Kick, Pull, Breathe, and Turn, No Support

Repeat Drill 6 but, after a few strokes, reach and pull to one side to effect a turn. Try to swim across the pool, make a wide turn, and return. Continue to breathe on every breathing-side arm pull while turning.

Success Goal = 2 round-trips without stopping

Your Score = (#) _____ round-trips without stopping

8. Deep-Water Pull, Kick, Breathe, and Turn

With your instructor watching, begin to swim and breathe at the shallow end. Swim to the deep end. Make a wide turn and return to the shallow end. Maintain a small kick.

Success Goal = 2 pool lengths or 120 to 150 total feet

Your Score = (#) _____ total feet

Pulling and Breathing Keys to Success Checklist

You have been testing yourself quantitatively by attaining each of the Step 11 Success Goals. It is time to look at your skills qualitatively as well. Ask someone who has a trained eye for detail in swimming to check the following items for quality and to suggest to you which items, if any, need further work to speed you on your way.

Preparation Phase

_____ Floats and pulls without support

Execution
Phase

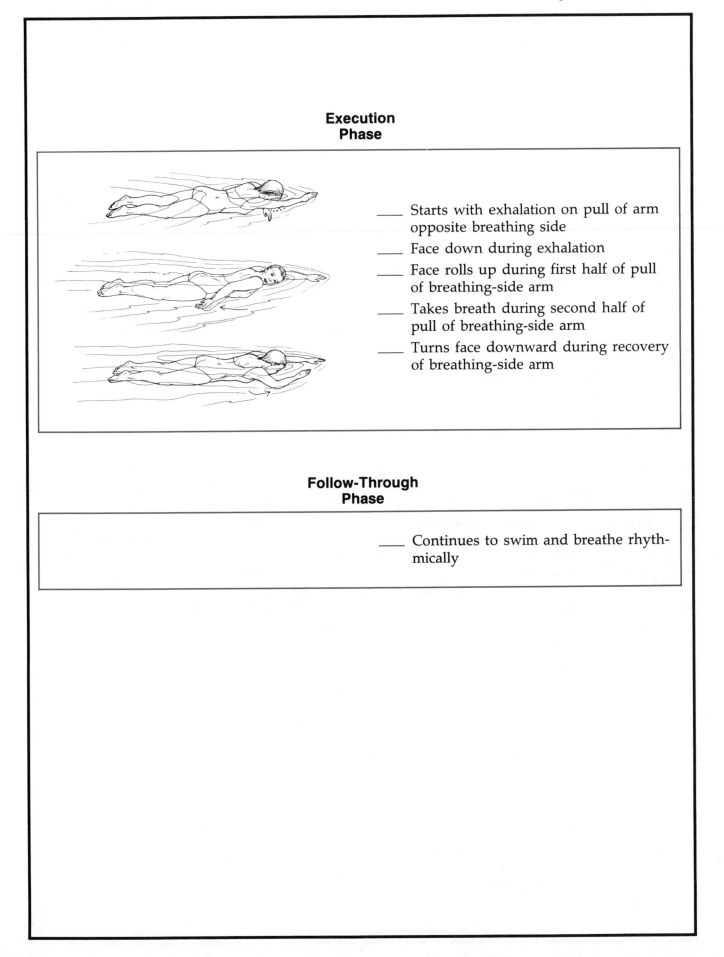

_____ Starts with exhalation on pull of arm opposite breathing side

_____ Face down during exhalation

_____ Face rolls up during first half of pull of breathing-side arm

_____ Takes breath during second half of pull of breathing-side arm

_____ Turns face downward during recovery of breathing-side arm

Follow-Through
Phase

_____ Continues to swim and breathe rhythmically

Step 12 Turning Over

You have learned to swim on your back. You have learned to swim in a prone position. You have learned to turn your head and shoulders to the side to breathe. An extension of this turn will allow you to go from a prone stroke to a backstroke.

WHY IS TURNING OVER IMPORTANT?

On occasion, especially when learning, you may inhale at the wrong time in a prone position and take in some water. If you were in deep water when this happened, the ability to roll over onto your back to rest, cough, and keep your face clear of the water for a few moments could be a lifesaver. In addition, the ability to roll your body at will is a necessary progression from the beginner arm stroke to the overarm stroke used in the crawl. You will see how floating on your side greatly facilitates breathing during an overhand arm recovery. If you learn this step well, you will have no difficulty with the crawl stroke.

HOW TO TURN OVER

With your breathing-side ankle in the loop of the deep leg support, pull through the water and breathe to the side. Do not try to kick, but keep your feet close together. On the third pull of your breathing-side arm, turn your head farther than usual and raise your chin. Pull your arm past your thigh and move the whole arm way back behind you. Let your arm guide you over onto your back. *Arch your back*; it is very important to arch, and to lift your hips into the back float position. Hold a big breath until you are steady in a back float, extending your arms beyond shoulder level. Relax. Breathe. Scull if you need support. Take a breath. Bring your breathing-side arm down to your hips and on across your body. Turn your head *away* from your breathing side, drop your chin, and bend slightly forward at the hips. Your body will roll into a facedown position. Continue pulling and breathing (see Figure 12.1).

Figure 12.1 Keys to Success: *Turning Over*

Preparation Phase

1. Pull and breathe with deep float
2. 3 strokes

Execution
Phase

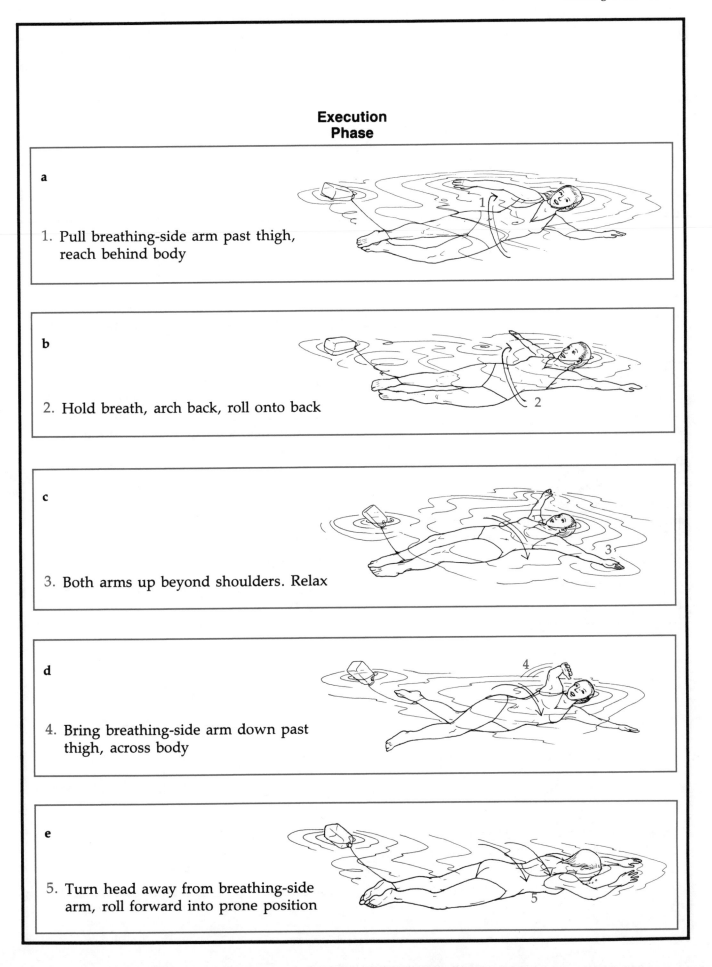

a

1. Pull breathing-side arm past thigh, reach behind body

b

2. Hold breath, arch back, roll onto back

c

3. Both arms up beyond shoulders. Relax

d

4. Bring breathing-side arm down past thigh, across body

e

5. Turn head away from breathing-side arm, roll forward into prone position

**Follow-Through
Phase**

1. Continue pulling

Detecting Errors in Turning Over

Learning to recognize a well-executed turnover is easier if you can compare correct and incorrect techniques. The most common errors in turning over are listed below, along with suggestions on how to correct them.

ERROR 🚫

CORRECTION

ERROR	CORRECTION
1. You fail to roll over onto back.	1. Raise chin. Arch back. Reach arm back.
2. You sink on back.	2. Take bigger breath, scull.
3. Water gets into your nose.	3. Exhale quickly as you roll, then take a big breath.

Turning Over Drills

1. Turnover Drill

In shallow water, practice turning over as described in Figure 12.1 until you can turn over consistently with confidence.

Success Goal = 8 successful front-to-back and back-to-front turnovers

Your Score = (#) _____ front-to-back and back-to-front turnovers

2. Turnovers Without Support

Float, pull, and kick without support. Turn over, front to back, and back to front. Keep your feet close together while turning over. Use a support kick while on your back.

Success Goal = 5 front-to-back turnovers and back-to-front turnovers

Your Score = (#) _____ turnovers in each direction

3. Deep-Water Turnover, Front to Back

With your instructor watching, start in shallow water and swim into deep water in a prone position. Make a wide turn and start back. Then turn over and swim back into shallow water using the back arm stroke and kick.

Success Goal = 3 round trips

Your Score = (#) _____ round trips

4. Deep-Water Turnover, Back to Front

With your instructor watching, start in shallow water and swim into deep water on your back. Make a wide turn. Then turn over to the front and return to shallow water in prone position, kicking and pulling.

Success Goal = 3 round trips

Your Score = (#) _____ round trips

5. Deep-Water Turnover and Rest

With your instructor watching, start at the shallow end of the pool and swim prone to the deep end (or 75 feet). Then make a wide turn and start back toward the shallow end. Turn over onto your back and rest as nearly motionless as possible. (Nonbuoyant persons may have to use a support kick, and possibly some sculling. All others should float motionless, resting, and concentrating on breathing.) After 30 full seconds of rest, kick your feet to the surface, turn over, and swim back to the starting point on your stomach.

Success Goal = Complete the drill twice or 2 successful round-trips

Your Score = (#) _____ round-trips

6. Swim and Rest for Distance

With your instructor watching, swim for distance. Swim continuously up and down the pool. Turn over onto your back to rest whenever you wish, for as long as you wish.

Success Goal = 100 yards

Your Score = (#) _____ yards

7. Front-to-Back Turnover Through the Vertical

In shoulder-deep water, swim in a prone position. Take a breath, hold it, and stop swimming. Press down with both hands on the water in front of you, raise your head, and tuck your knees under you; this will cause your feet to drop directly down. When your feet are under you, arch your back, put your head back, scull, and step up to the surface by extending your toes and pressing alternately as in the support kick. You should make an easy transition *through the vertical* to a back-swimming position.

Success Goal = 5 successful front-to-back vertical transitions

Your Score = (#) _____ front-to-back vertical transitions

8. Back-to-Front Turnover Through the Vertical

In shoulder-deep water, swim on your back. Take a deep breath and stop swimming. "Sit" up and tuck your feet under you. Put your face forward into the water, extend one foot be-

hind you as far as you can reach, and press down on the water with the top of this foot. Then step back with the other foot as far as you can reach and press down on the water with the top of this foot. Reach out in front of you and start your arm pull. You should make the transition from back to front easily *through the vertical position.*

Success Goal = 5 successful back-to-front vertical transitions

Your Score = (#) _____ back-to-front vertical transitions

Turning Over
Keys to Success Checklist

Turning over successfully and turning over nicely may be two different things. You have turned over successfully—now ask a knowledgeable person to evaluate your skill in turning over from a qualitative standpoint. Smooth execution and precision may be determined by using the following checklist.

**Preparation
Phase**

____ Smooth pulling and breathing with deep leg float
____ 3 long, full pulls

Execution
Phase

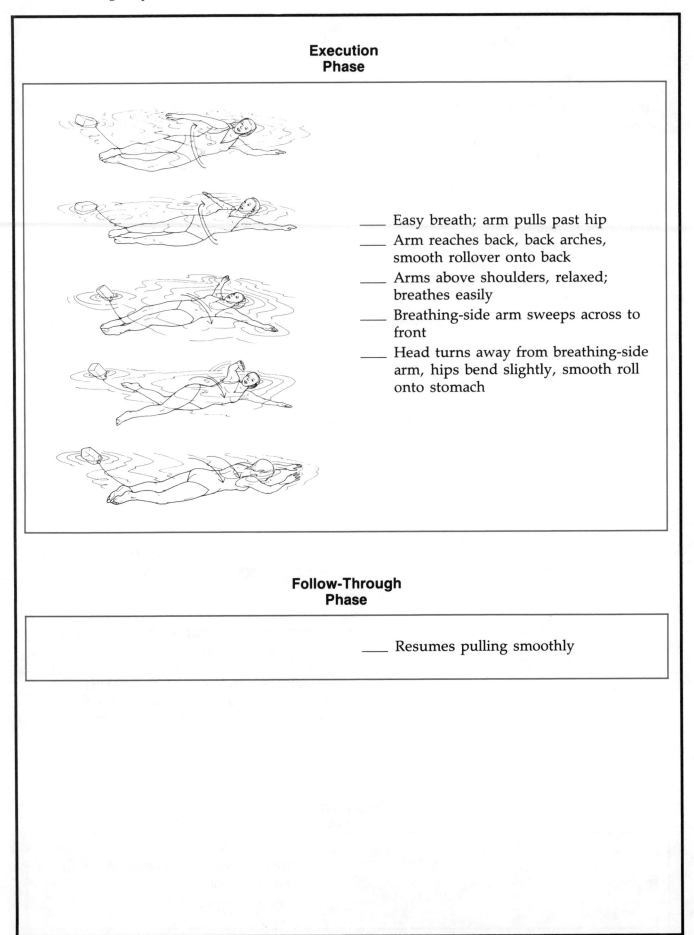

____ Easy breath; arm pulls past hip

____ Arm reaches back, back arches, smooth rollover onto back

____ Arms above shoulders, relaxed; breathes easily

____ Breathing-side arm sweeps across to front

____ Head turns away from breathing-side arm, hips bend slightly, smooth roll onto stomach

Follow-Through
Phase

____ Resumes pulling smoothly

Step 13 **Side Glide**

By this time you should be feeling quite confident of your ability to swim. However, you may be frustrated because you haven't yet learned what most people regard as "real" swimming—that is, the overhand, or crawl, stroke. This step is your final preparation before learning the overhand arm motion.

WHY IS THE SIDE GLIDE IMPORTANT?

We are fortunate in being able to assume virtually any position we wish while floating in the water. We do it by balancing our weight around the center of buoyancy in the body, the lungs. Being able to feel and adjust the balance of your body to attain any desired position is a vital part of water proficiency.

The side glide is worth learning just for its contribution to your overall safety in the water, but it is important for another reason, also. This specific skill is the position from which the overhand arm motion must be made if you wish to swim smoothly and expertly and breathe without stress. The key to the side glide is balance. If you arch your back, you will float over onto your back. If you bend forward at the hips, you will float face down. If your body is stretched, subtle variations in the bend of your hips or arch of your back will allow you to maintain a side float position.

HOW TO EXECUTE THE SIDE GLIDE

Swim in the prone position. While pulling through with your breathing-side arm, turn your body onto your side to breathe. Stop with your breathing-side arm resting on your side and your opposite arm stretched beyond your head. Keep your ear pressed tightly to your forward arm and hold this side glide for about 3 or 4 seconds. Return to the prone position and resume stroking. Roll onto the opposite side while pulling with the opposite arm. Take a breath and hold a side glide on that side for 3 or 4 seconds, also. Continue, stopping and gliding on each side (see Figure 13.1).

Figure 13.1 Keys to Success: **Side Glide**

**Preparation
Phase**

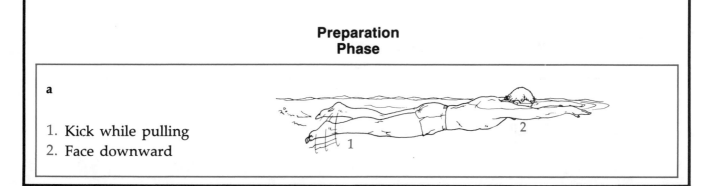

a

1. Kick while pulling
2. Face downward

Execution
Phase

b

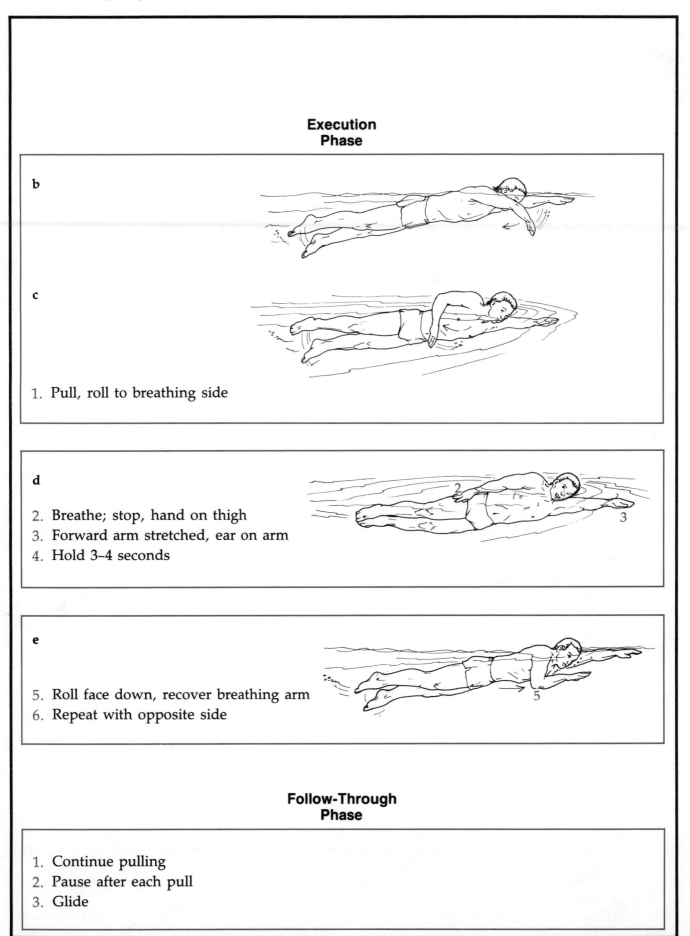

c

1. Pull, roll to breathing side

d

2. Breathe; stop, hand on thigh
3. Forward arm stretched, ear on arm
4. Hold 3–4 seconds

e

5. Roll face down, recover breathing arm
6. Repeat with opposite side

Follow-Through
Phase

1. Continue pulling
2. Pause after each pull
3. Glide

Detecting Errors in the Side Glide

Learning to recognize errors in the side glide is easier if you can compare correct and incorrect techniques. The most common errors in performing the side glide are listed below, along with suggestions on how to correct them.

ERROR 🚫

CORRECTION

ERROR	CORRECTION
1. You roll facedown.	1. Arch your back slightly.
2. You roll onto back.	2. Bend slightly forward at hips.
3. Body sinks.	3. Take a deeper breath. Keep rear arm underwater against side.
4. Feet sink.	4. Hold glide only until forward motion slows. Keep ear pressed against lower arm.
5. Head sinks.	5. Keep forward arm under head.
6. You inhale water.	6. Roll slightly more onto back. Keep ear pressed against lower arm.

Side Glide Drills

1. Side Glide From Push-Off With Leg Support

Use a deep float leg support on your breathing-side ankle. Hold the edge of the pool with your breathing-side hand. Turn sideways to the pool wall, extend your opposite arm out toward open water, put both feet against the wall near the top, and lay your ear on the free, forward arm. Take a deep breath and push off from the wall on your side, extending and streamlining your body. Keep your trailing

arm against your side and glide as long as possible. Control your balance on your side by bending very slightly at your hips as needed. Breathe deeply and hold each breath.

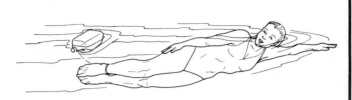

Success Goal = 30 seconds floating on your side

Your Score = (#) _____ seconds

2. Opposite Side Glide

Attach a deep leg support to the other leg and repeat Drill 1 on the opposite side. Do not lift your head; keep your ear in the water.

Success Goal = 30 seconds floating on your side

Your Score = (#) _____ seconds

3. Side Glide, No Support

Push off from the side in side glide position with no float support. Glide only as long as your feet remain near the surface. Concentrate on balancing in the side position. Lay your head down. Glide on each side.

Success Goal = 4 glides on each side without rolling

Your Score = (#) _____ glides without rolling

4. Pull and Side Glide, Breathing Side Only

Attach a deep float leg support to the ankle on your breathing side. Start pulling in the prone position. Beginning with the third stroke of your breathing arm, pull the arm to your side and roll into a side glide. Keep your ear in the water. Hold the glide for only 4 seconds before resuming your stroking. However, stop in the side glide position for 4 seconds *every time* your breathing arm pulls.

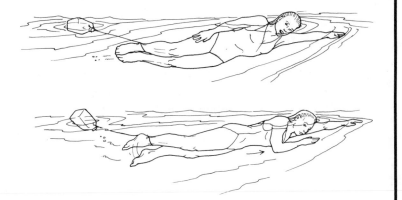

Success Goal = 5 consecutive breathing-side glides for 4 seconds each

Your Score = (#) _____ breathing-side glides

5. Pull and Side Glide Non-Breathing Side Only

Attach a deep float to the ankle of your non-breathing side. Change your breathing pattern to breathe on the opposite side for this drill. The side glide will give you plenty of time to get a breath, even though it seems awkward. You will need a little practice to get used to this new breathing pattern. Pull and stop to breathe in a side glide each time the new breathing-side arm reaches your hip.

Success Goal = 5 consecutive opposite side glides for 4 seconds each

Your Score = (#) _____ opposite side glides

6. *Pull and Side Glide Combination*

Repeat Drills 4 and 5 without a leg support. Kick gently for leg support while stroking, but stop all motion for the glide. Cut the glide time to 3 seconds.

Success Goal = 5 consecutive side glides on each side for 3 seconds each

Your Score = (#) _____ side glides on each side

7. *Two-Second Glide*

While swimming with a small kick in a prone position, pull into a side glide with *each* arm stroke. Hold each glide for only 2 seconds, but make a definite stop and glide. Breathe only on your usual breathing side; turn your shoulders and body to a side glide position on your opposite side, but keep your face turned into the water on that side. Stroke slowly and make each stroke full and deliberate. Adjust your breathing to the slower pace required.

Success Goal = 10 consecutive arm strokes with 2-second glides, done in an easy, relaxed manner

Your Score = (#) _____ arm strokes with glides

Side Glide Keys To Success Checklist

You have been proving yourself quantitatively by attaining each of the Step 13 Success Goals. Next ask your teacher, coach, or a trained observer to evaluate your technique qualitatively according to the checklist below. He or she may decide to create an individual practice program for you.

Preparation Phase

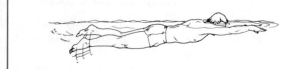

_____ Kicking and pulling, prone position

Execution
Phase

____ Rolls to breathing side while pulling

____ Takes a breath, and stops in side glide position; trailing hand rests relaxed on thigh

____ Ear is underwater, resting on extended forward arm

____ Holds side glide 3–4 seconds

____ Rolls face down, recovers breathing arm

____ Repeats the drill on the opposite side

Follow-Through
Phase

____ Resumes stroking smoothly; stops, glides on each pull

Step 14 Overhand Arm Stroke

Now it is finally time to do some "real" swimming. You have all the prerequisites for doing the overhand stroke. Not only are you ready, but it must have been difficult *not* to recover your arm over the water from your side glide position. It seems so natural at this point that it will be an easy transition for you. Please remember, though, that you cannot have *both* an arm *and* your mouth out at the same time without some additional support. The overhand stroke requires precise timing in order to allow you to breathe when the breathing-side arm is *not* out of water.

WHY IS THE OVERHAND STROKE IMPORTANT?

The overhand stroke is important to you because it will allow you, for the first time, to employ the pull with no underwater resistance on the recovery. You will not save much energy, because it requires as much energy to lift an arm over the surface as to push it through the water, but you will gain a great deal of efficiency (you'll move farther and faster) for the same effort.

HOW TO DO THE OVERHAND (CRAWL) ARM STROKE

In the side glide position, allow your trailing hand to rest on your thigh, but turn it *palm up*. Recover by lifting your elbow. Allow your hand to be fully relaxed, fingers trailing at the surface. Your elbow should bend about 90 degrees and lead your hand until your arm is at shoulder height. Stay in the side glide position and keep your elbow higher than your hand as your hand passes your face. Reach forward with your hand but keep your shoulder and elbow up. Place your hand in the water as far in front as you can reach, but bend your arm as if you were reaching over a barrel lying on its side in front of your head. Your fingertips should touch the water before your elbow. Roll your face down and glide on this arm as you begin your pull with your opposite arm. Repeat the roll and arm action on the other side, except that your face should stay underwater. Do not allow the position of your face to keep you from rolling fully to your side in this other direction. Stay on your side until your hand passes your head, with high elbow to reach "over the barrel" on this side now (see Figure 14.1).

Figure 14.1 Keys to Success: *Overhand Arm Stroke*

Preparation Phase

1. Pull into side glide position

**Execution
Phase**

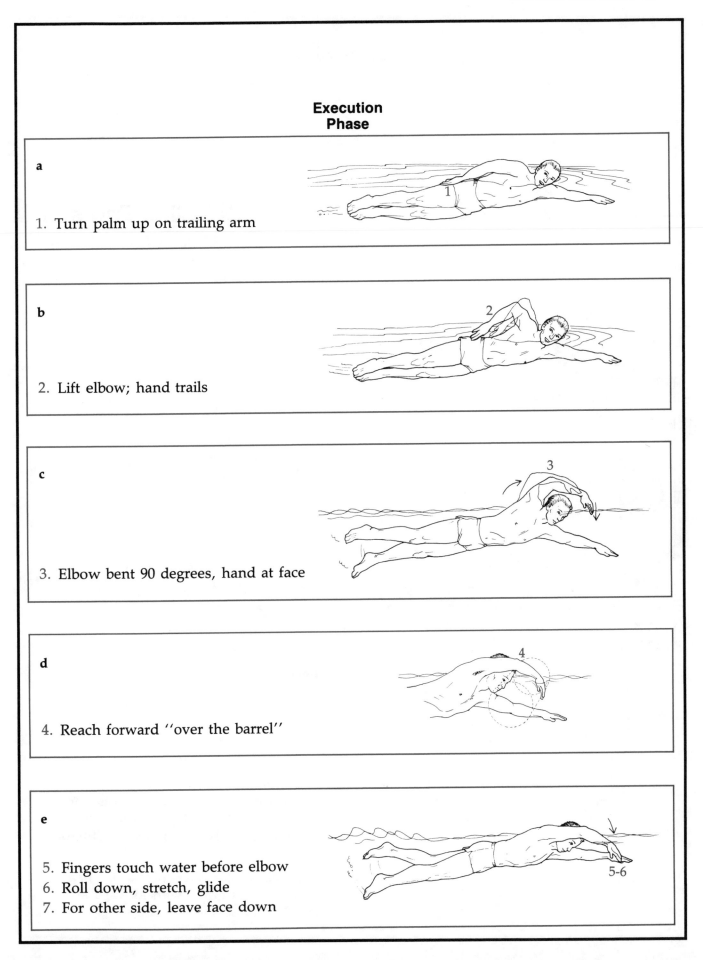

a

1. Turn palm up on trailing arm

b

2. Lift elbow; hand trails

c

3. Elbow bent 90 degrees, hand at face

d

4. Reach forward "over the barrel"

e

5. Fingers touch water before elbow
6. Roll down, stretch, glide
7. For other side, leave face down

**Follow-Through
Phase**

1. Alternate arms
2. Breathe on one side only

Detecting Errors in the Overhand Stroke

Learning to recognize a well-executed overhand stroke is easier if you can compare correct and incorrect techniques. The most common overhand stroke errors are listed below, along with suggestions on how to correct them.

ERROR 🚫

CORRECTION

1. You take in water when trying to breathe.

1. Do not try to breathe when arm is out of water; breathe during last half of *pull*.

2. Elbow touches water before fingertips.

2. Stay in side glide position longer. Keep shoulder high.

3. Elbow drops, hand leads.

3. Relax wrist and trail fingertips along surface of water.

4. Hand is palm down.

4. Finish pull with palm up.

5. Hand enters at head.

5. Reach forward over the barrel.

6. Lower arm pulls during recovery of upper arm.

6. Any pulling with the lower arm during the recovery of the upper arm is done for support. Instead, the lower arm should be used as a runner to glide on (see Touch-and-Go Drills 4, 5, 6).

7. Feet sink.

7. Keep ear underwater, do not lift head. Do not press down with forward arm and hand.

Overhand Stroke Drills

1. Overhand Drill, Breathing Side, Supported

Use a deep float leg support on your breathing-side ankle. Hold a kickboard in your opposite hand, your fingers on top of the board and your thumb underneath. Assume a side glide position, your ear on your extended forward arm. Go through the motions of the overhand recovery in slow motion; watch your recovering arm. Roll onto your stomach as your hand enters the water. Stretch your breathing-side arm forward as you exhale. Pull. Inhale during the last half of the pull. Stop and float in side glide position. Repeat, using only your breathing-side arm again and again.

Success Goal = 10 consecutive strokes with breathing-side arm

Your Score = (#) _____ strokes

2. Overhand Stroke, Side Opposite Breathing Side, Supported

Repeat Drill 1 on your other side. Keep your face out of the water during the recovery, so you can see your arm motion. Attach the float to your other ankle (on your upper leg), keep your lower ear underwater, and exhale as your hand enters the water and stretches. Inhale on the last half of the pull. Use only the non-breathing-side arm. Perform drill again and again.

Success Goal = 10 consecutive strokes with the arm on the non-breathing side

Your Score = (#) _____ strokes

3. Overhand Stroke, Both Arms, Supported

Start as above, using the leg float on either ankle. As your recovering arm reaches forward, take hold of the kickboard with that hand and release it from the other hand. Now pull and recover with your free arm. Keep changing hands with the kickboard as each arm reaches forward. Breathe *only* on your regular breathing side. Keep your face in the water during the recovery of the opposite arm. Exhale during the pull of the non-breathing-side arm. Try to move in slow motion. Keep your feet fairly close together. Do not "swim"—just *float* along and pull with both arms alternately.

Success Goal = 10 consecutive strokes, 5 with each arm

Your Score = (#) _____ strokes with each arm

4. Touch-and-Go Overhand Stroke Drill, Leg Support

Repeat Drill 3, but without the kickboard. Use the leg support float again. Start pulling with the arm opposite your breathing-side arm. Exhale. Be sure to keep your forward arm straight and stretched until the recovering hand stretches forward and touches it. Thus "touch" the forward hand to tell it when to "go." Continue touch-and-go alternate overhand stroking. Breathe only on your regular breathing side, but breathe *every time* that arm pulls. Breathe on the pull, *not* on the recovery.

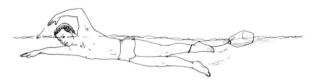

Success Goal = 10 consecutive touch-and-go strokes, 5 with each arm

Your Score = (#) _____ touch-and-go strokes with each arm

5. Touch-and-Go Overhand Stroke Drill, Unsupported

Repeat Drill 4 without the leg support. Use a small kick in whatever rhythm is comfortable.

Success Goal = 10 touch-and-go strokes, 5 with each arm

Your Score = (#) _____ touch-and-go strokes with each arm

6. Touch-and-Go Overhand Stroke for Distance

Go across the pool in shallow water. Without the leg support, continue the overhand touch-and-go stroke, breathing on the breathing side only. Turn when you get close to a wall and keep going for distance; do not count strokes.

Success Goal = 3 pool widths without stopping

Your Score = (#) _____ pool widths

7. Deep-Water Overhand Stroke

With your instructor watching, start at the deep end of the pool and swim an overhand stroke to the shallow end. Continue with the touch-and-go style.

Success Goal = one pool length or 75 feet

Your Score = (#) _____ feet

8. Overhand Stroke With Mask and Snorkel

With your instructor watching, don mask and snorkel and use the overhand stroke to swim the length of the pool, starting at the deep end. Remember to keep your face in the water, but turn your body into the side float position for the arm recovery on each side.

Success Goal = one pool length with 100 percent *good* overhand recoveries

Your Score = _____ percent *good* arm recoveries (your judgment)

9. Deep-Water Overhand Stroke for Distance

Use no equipment, but have your instructor watch. Start at the shallow end of the pool. Swim to the deep end of the pool, make a wide turn, and swim back to the shallow end. Use the overhand stroke only.

Success Goal = 2 lengths of the pool or 150 feet

Your Score = (#) _____ feet

10. Overhand Stroke and Deep-Water Turnover

With your instructor watching, start at the shallow end of the pool with no equipment. Swim to the deep end, make a wide turn, and start back. Part of the way back, turn onto your back and float with slow sculling and a support kick. After one minute, turn over again and swim to the shallow end using an overhand stroke.

Success Goal = 2 lengths with an easy, restful interval

Your Score = _____ completed (yes or no)?

Overhand Stroke Keys to Success Checklist

Most of the drills have goals quantified in terms of number of repetitions or distance necessary to master each skill, but it is difficult to measure something like an arm recovery on a quantitative basis. You may have noticed that some drills now require subjective judgments on your part. Refer now to a qualified expert who can judge your skill qualitatively using the checklist below as a guide.

Preparation Phase

_____ Inhales while pulling easily into side glide

Execution
Phase

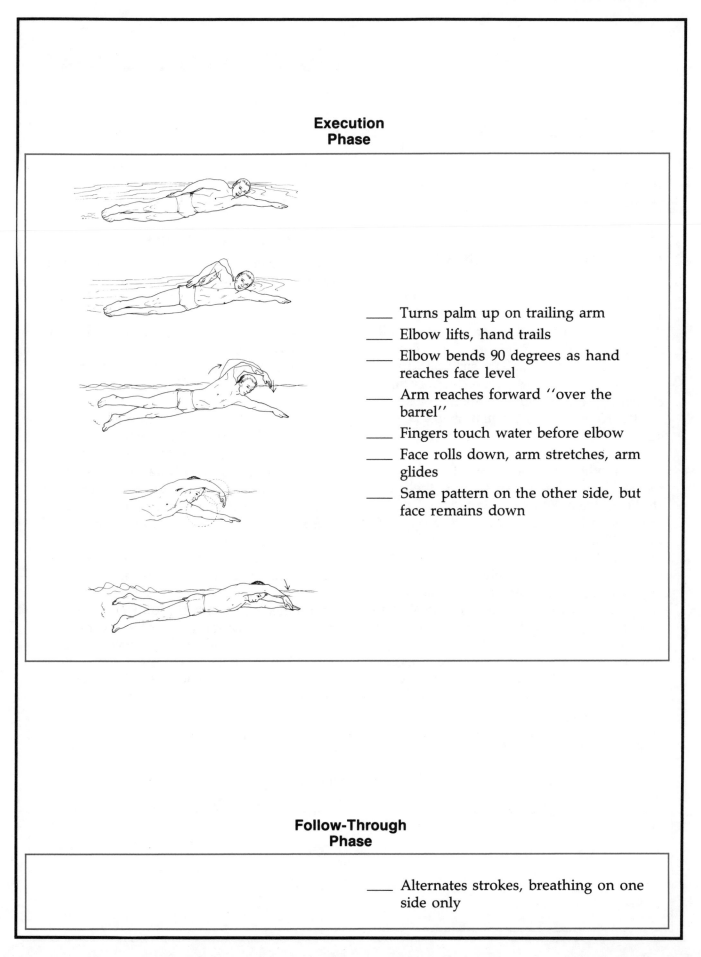

_____ Turns palm up on trailing arm

_____ Elbow lifts, hand trails

_____ Elbow bends 90 degrees as hand reaches face level

_____ Arm reaches forward "over the barrel"

_____ Fingers touch water before elbow

_____ Face rolls down, arm stretches, arm glides

_____ Same pattern on the other side, but face remains down

Follow-Through
Phase

_____ Alternates strokes, breathing on one side only

Step 15 **Crawl Stroke**

Here it is at last—"real" swimming! Now you'll package an arm stroke, a leg kick, and a breathing pattern into a "name" stroke! The crawl is the most efficient and fastest stroke known. With only a few modifications of the techniques you have been using, *you* can swim the crawl.

WHY IS THE CRAWL STROKE IMPORTANT?

The crawl stroke is the very essence of the image of "swimming." It will move you through the water faster than any other stroke, while allowing you to see where you are going. It will not save energy, and for survival you will turn to other strokes. It *uses* energy most efficiently—it does not *save* energy most efficiently. Nevertheless, it will probably be your stroke of choice anytime you decide to go swimming.

Two modifications are necessary to combine the skills you have learned into the crawl stroke package. You must start the pull of one arm just prior to the entry of the opposite hand, thus eliminating the "touch" of the touch-and-go stroke. You must also modify your kick somewhat, timing the kick to the arm stroke so that you have 6 kicks to each complete arm-stroke cycle (both arms). This 6-beat (-kick) crawl stroke is still considered to be the standard crawl stroke, although other timing combinations are acceptable. This step will teach the 6-beat stroke but allow you to

adopt whatever rhythm you desire. The kick is more important for balance than for propulsion.

This step will describe the stroke, then use drills to lead you progressively through the modifications you will have to make.

HOW TO SWIM THE CRAWL STROKE

Starting from the prone float position, begin kicking, counting each downward thrust of each foot. Count in sets of 6 kicks. Emphasize counts 1 and 4 thus: **1**-2-3-**4**-5-6. After two complete sets of kicks, begin the pull of the arm opposite your breathing side on the count of **1**. Pull completely through, exhale, and recover on the counts of 2 and 3. As you count 3, your recovering hand should be passing your head on the way to entering the water, your elbow bent high. On the count of **4**, your recovering hand drops into the water, fingertips first, and your breathing-side arm simultaneously begins its pull. On the counts of 5 and 6, your breathing-side arm pulls through; you breathe on the last half of the pull; and your arm recovers to the level of your head, ready to enter the water, elbow held high. On the count of **1**, your breathing-side hand enters the water, fingertips first, and you simultaneously begin the pull with the opposite arm. Recapping: your hands enter the water on counts **1** and **4**. You exhale on counts 2 and 3 and inhale on counts 5 and 6. Your feet kick steadily, with no hesitation or change in rhythm (see Figure 15.1).

Figure 15.1 Keys to Success: Crawl Stroke

**Preparation
Phase**

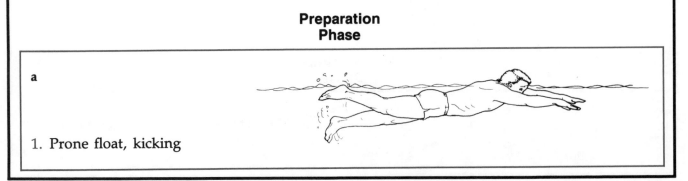

a

1. Prone float, kicking

**Execution
Phase**

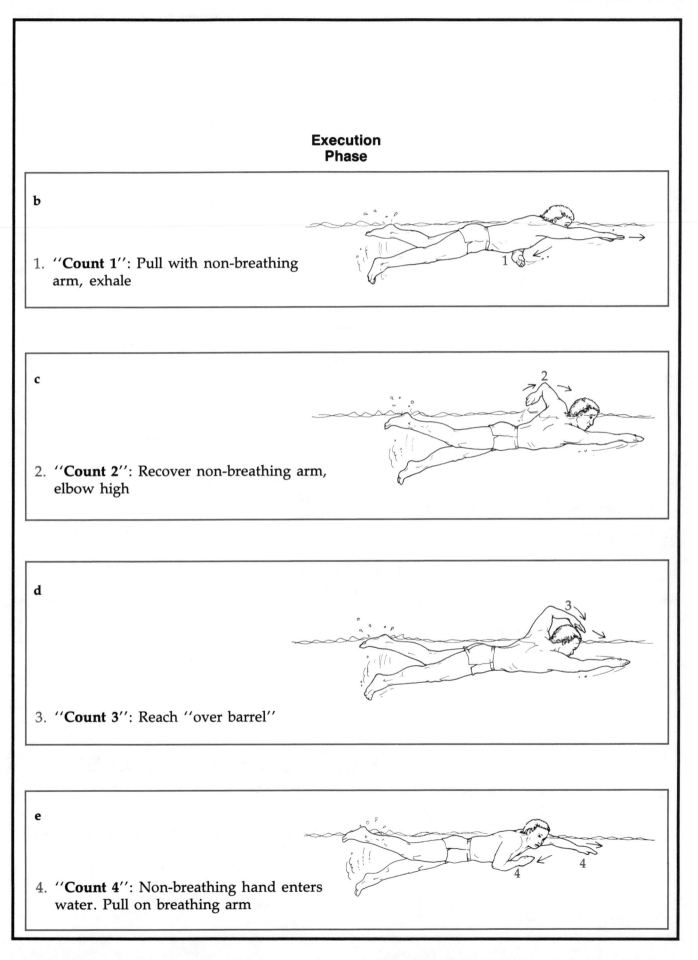

b

1. **"Count 1"**: Pull with non-breathing arm, exhale

c

2. **"Count 2"**: Recover non-breathing arm, elbow high

d

3. **"Count 3"**: Reach "over barrel"

e

4. **"Count 4"**: Non-breathing hand enters water. Pull on breathing arm

f

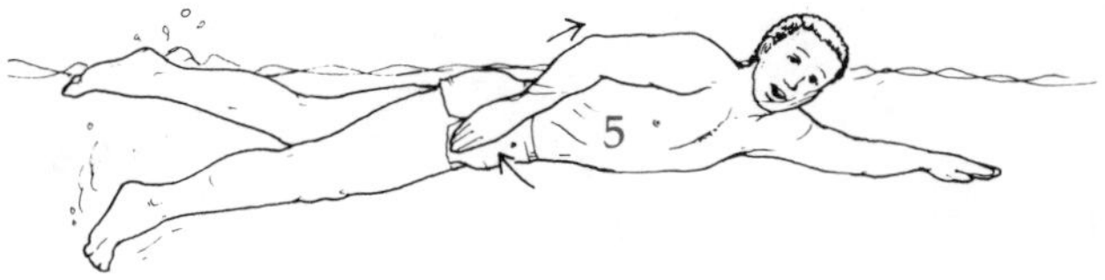

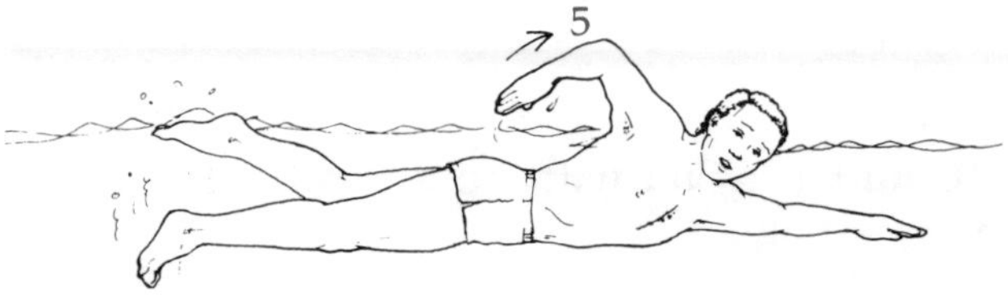

5. "**Count 5**": Inhale on last half of pull; recover breathing arm, elbow high

g

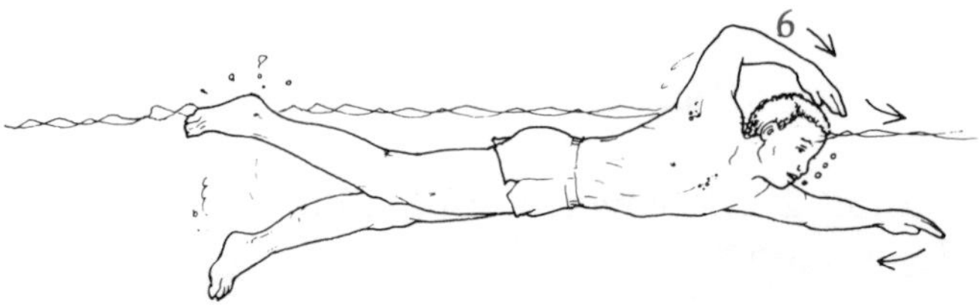

6. "**Count 6**": Reach "over barrel"

Follow-Through Phase

1. Continue rhythmically

Detecting Errors in Crawl Stroke

Learning to recognize a well-executed crawl stroke is easier if you can compare correct and incorrect techniques. The most common crawl stroke errors are listed below, along with suggestions on how to correct them.

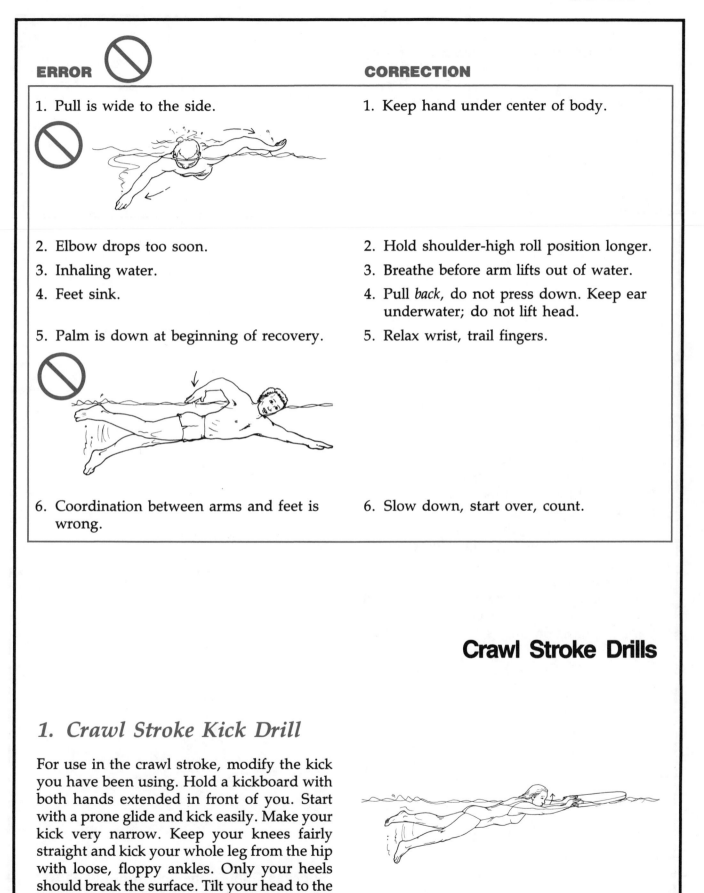

ERROR	CORRECTION
1. Pull is wide to the side.	1. Keep hand under center of body.
2. Elbow drops too soon.	2. Hold shoulder-high roll position longer.
3. Inhaling water.	3. Breathe before arm lifts out of water.
4. Feet sink.	4. Pull *back*, do not press down. Keep ear underwater; do not lift head.
5. Palm is down at beginning of recovery.	5. Relax wrist, trail fingers.
6. Coordination between arms and feet is wrong.	6. Slow down, start over, count.

Crawl Stroke Drills

1. Crawl Stroke Kick Drill

For use in the crawl stroke, modify the kick you have been using. Hold a kickboard with both hands extended in front of you. Start with a prone glide and kick easily. Make your kick very narrow. Keep your knees fairly straight and kick your whole leg from the hip with loose, floppy ankles. Only your heels should break the surface. Tilt your head to the front to inhale; drop your face into the water to exhale. Count each downward kick, *beginning your count with the leg on your breathing side*; and count in sets of 6, with emphasis on the counts of **1** and **4**. Kick for propulsion. If your ankles are stiff and toes do not point well, you will get very little forward movement. You should, however, be able to get enough support to keep your feet near the surface. Pressing too hard on the kickboard will make your feet sink.

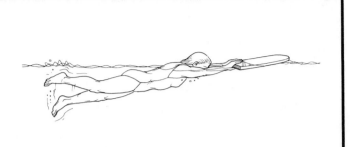

Success Goal = one pool width or 45 feet

Your Score = (#) _____ feet

2. Crawl Kick With Swim Fins, Kickboard

Don a pair of swim fins. Bring to class a pair of athletic socks to wear in the swim fins to prevent chafing by fins that may not fit exactly. Repeat Drill 1 with the fins. Do not try to kick the fins; kick your legs from the hips and let the fins do whatever they wish. Your ankles *must* be relaxed so the fins can flop properly to furnish propulsion. Try to keep your knees fairly straight. Flutter your relaxed feet. You will be aware of a tremendous increase in propulsion. Count your kicks in groups of 6, with emphasis on counts **1** and **4**, *beginning with the leg on your breathing side*.

Success Goal = one pool width or 45 feet

Your Score = (#) _____ feet

3. Crawl Kick With Fins, Breathing-Side Pull

Wearing fins, but without the kickboard, begin to kick as above. Exhale underwater on the first set of 6 kicks. On the second set of 6 kicks, begin to pull on the count of **4** with your breathing arm only. Use the overhand stroke recovery. Roll and breathe as you pull on counts **4**, 5, and 6. Return the arm to the water on count **1**. Exhale as you glide on counts **1**, 2, and 3 with your arms stretched overhead. Pull and breathe again on your breathing side on counts **4**, 5, and 6, returning your arm to the water on count **1**. Continue, pulling only on your breathing side. Roll fully into the side glide position to facilitate breathing, but do not pause in the side glide position. Continue the rhythm of the kick.

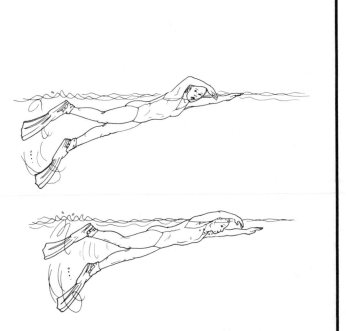

Success Goal = one pool width or 45 feet

Your Score = (#) _____ feet

4. Crawl Kick, Breathing-Side Pull, No Aids

Repeat Drill 3 without the fins. Propulsion from the kick will be minimal, and you will have to rely more on the arm pull for propulsion. Keep the kick small and work on making exact coordination between leg counts and arm movements. Slow down your movements so you can float along, concentrating your attention on the counting.

Success Goal = 10 breathing-side pulls with proper leg coordination

Your Score = (#) _____ pulls in proper coordination

5. Crawl Arm Pull, No Kick

Start with a prone glide, pulling alternately and breathing on your side, but do *not* kick your feet. Let your feet float along but keep them fairly close together. Count to 6 on each complete pull of both arms *as if* you were kicking. Concentrate on starting each pull on counts **1** and **4**. Concentrate on returning one hand to the water at the same time the next arm starts its pull. Use your deep float leg support if you wish.

Success Goal = 5 complete arm pulls with proper coordination

Your Score = (#) _____ complete arm pulls

6. *Coordinated Crawl Stroke*

Begin with a prone glide. Begin kicking with the foot on your breathing side. Count through a full sequence of 6 kicks while exhaling. Begin pulling and breathing on the second count of **4**. As your arm returns to the water on count **1**, begin the pull of the arm opposite your breathing side as you exhale. Be sure to return that arm to the water exactly on the count of **4**, as you begin the second pull of your breathing-side arm. Slow down to slow motion, just floating along and concentrating on the coordination between arms and legs.

Success Goal = 5 completely coordinated strokes with both arms

Your Score = (#) _____ coordinated strokes

7. *"Hesitation" Crawl Stroke*

Begin swimming a completely coordinated crawl stroke. On the second or third stroke, pause on the count of 3 in a side glide position with your breathing-side hand resting on your thigh and your kick stopped. Resume after a pause of 2 seconds. Pause again on the count of 6 in a side glide position on your opposite side, with your hand resting on your thigh, but your face down. Resume again after 2 seconds. Continue to swim this "hesitation" stroke, stopping all motion for 2 seconds on counts 3 and 6.

Success Goal = 10 consecutive arm strokes (5 on each side) with a hesitation in side glide position

Your Score = (#) _____ strokes with hesitation

8. *Crawl Stroke and Turn*

Begin swimming an easy crawl stroke across the pool. Near the opposite side, reach to the side and pull into a wide turn. Swim back to the starting point.

Success Goal = 180-degree turn without stopping

Your Score = _____ turn completed (yes or no)?

9. *Deep-Water Crawl Stroke*

With your instructor watching, begin at the shallow end of the pool, swim the crawl stroke to the deep end, make a wide turn, and swim back to the shallow end.

Success Goal = 2 lengths or 150 feet with a wide turn

Your Score = (#) _____ feet with a wide turn

10. Crawl Stroke for Distance

With your instructor watching, begin swimming the crawl stroke at the shallow end of the pool. Swim to the deep end, grasp the edge, tuck your feet, and turn your body around. Place your feet against the wall, put both hands in front of you, put your face down, and push off. Glide for 2 seconds before resuming the crawl stroke. Swim back to the shallow end, repeat the turn and push-off, and continue swimming lengths.

Success Goal = 4 pool lengths or 100 yards

Your Score = (#) _____ yards

Crawl Stroke Keys to Success Checklist

Numbers of strokes and yards swum are important measures of accomplishment, but how well you swim them is also important. Ease, fluidity, and rhythm are best evaluated qualitatively. Ask your instructor to make such an evaluation of your stroke using the following checklist.

Preparation Phase

_____ Easy, relaxed prone float position; counting rhythmic kicks

**Execution
Phase**

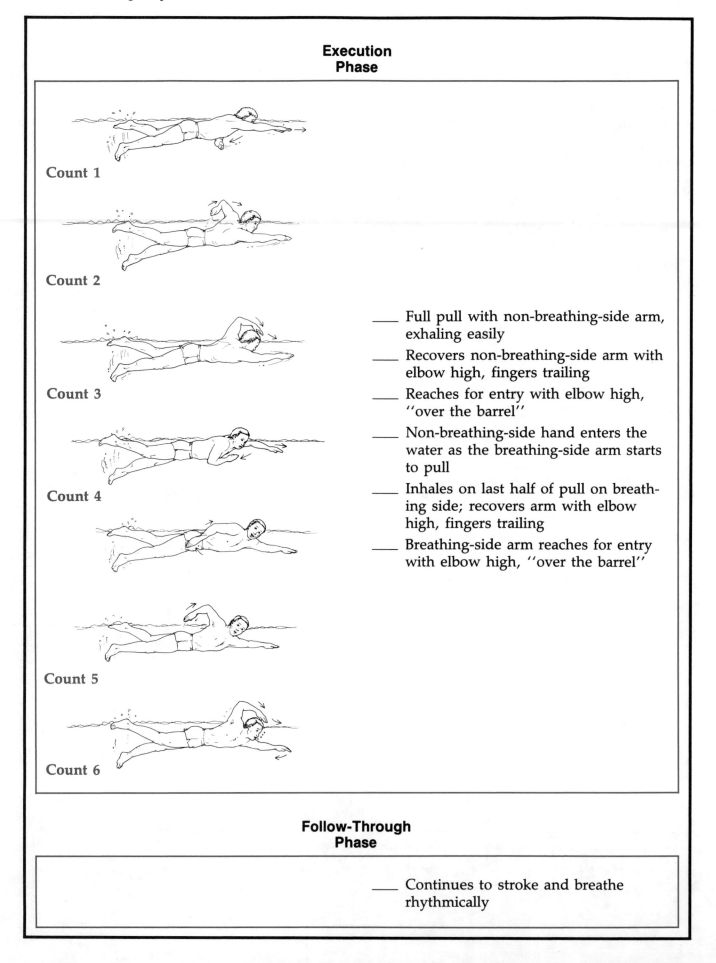

Count 1

Count 2

Count 3

Count 4

Count 5

Count 6

____ Full pull with non-breathing-side arm, exhaling easily

____ Recovers non-breathing-side arm with elbow high, fingers trailing

____ Reaches for entry with elbow high, "over the barrel"

____ Non-breathing-side hand enters the water as the breathing-side arm starts to pull

____ Inhales on last half of pull on breathing side; recovers arm with elbow high, fingers trailing

____ Breathing-side arm reaches for entry with elbow high, "over the barrel"

**Follow-Through
Phase**

____ Continues to stroke and breathe rhythmically

Step 16 Elementary Backstroke

The elementary backstroke is similar to the backstroke you have been swimming; in fact, the arm stroke is identical. The leg kick and timing are quite different, however; an entirely new foot and leg motion are introduced in this stroke.

WHY IS THE ELEMENTARY BACKSTROKE IMPORTANT?

The elementary backstroke is one of the recognized "package" strokes because of its ease and efficiency. It is efficient not for the *use* of energy, but for the *conservation* of energy. Its greater importance, however, lies in the fact that it is the most efficient way to introduce the breaststroke kick. We have been minimizing the importance of the kick in the strokes introduced to this point; however, in strokes that use the breaststroke kick (elementary backstroke and breaststroke), the kick produces as much propulsion as the arms.

The breaststroke kick is a unique motion. You should be cautioned against vigorous practice of the kick until your muscles and joints have time to adjust. Its efficiency depends upon the flexibility in your knees and ankles.

HOW TO SWIM THE ELEMENTARY BACKSTROKE

From a back float position, begin the recovery of your arms (as in Step 4). As your arms recover, drop your heels down, with your feet fully hooked toward your knees. Do not "sit," or bend at the hips. As your hands turn outward for the arm extension, your feet—still hooked—should be turned outward as far as possible. Your knees will separate somewhat to achieve this position, but they should stay fairly close to each other. As your arms stretch outward, move your feet out toes-first wider than your knees. As you begin to pull, your feet continue to move outward. The knees now separate, still bent to maximum flexion, your toes are turned out, and your feet are fully hooked. In midpull, push backward and squeeze in a circular motion with the inside of your hooked foot and ankle. Your ankle extends, and your toes point at the very end of the kick. The kick and arm stroke finish at about the same time, but your arms may finish just slightly after the kick. Remain streamlined but relaxed for a long glide (see Figure 16.1).

Figure 16.1 Keys to Success: *Elementary Backstroke*

**Preparation
Phase**

1. Back float position

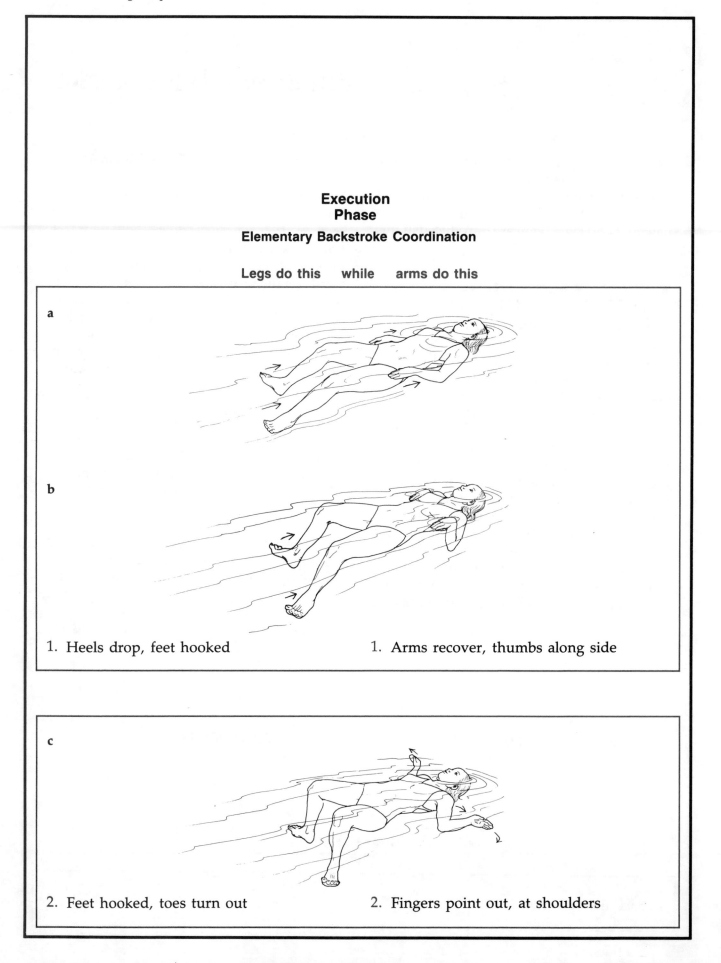

**Execution
Phase**

Elementary Backstroke Coordination

Legs do this   while   arms do this

a

b

1. Heels drop, feet hooked

1. Arms recover, thumbs along side

c

2. Feet hooked, toes turn out

2. Fingers point out, at shoulders

Legs do this   while   arms do this

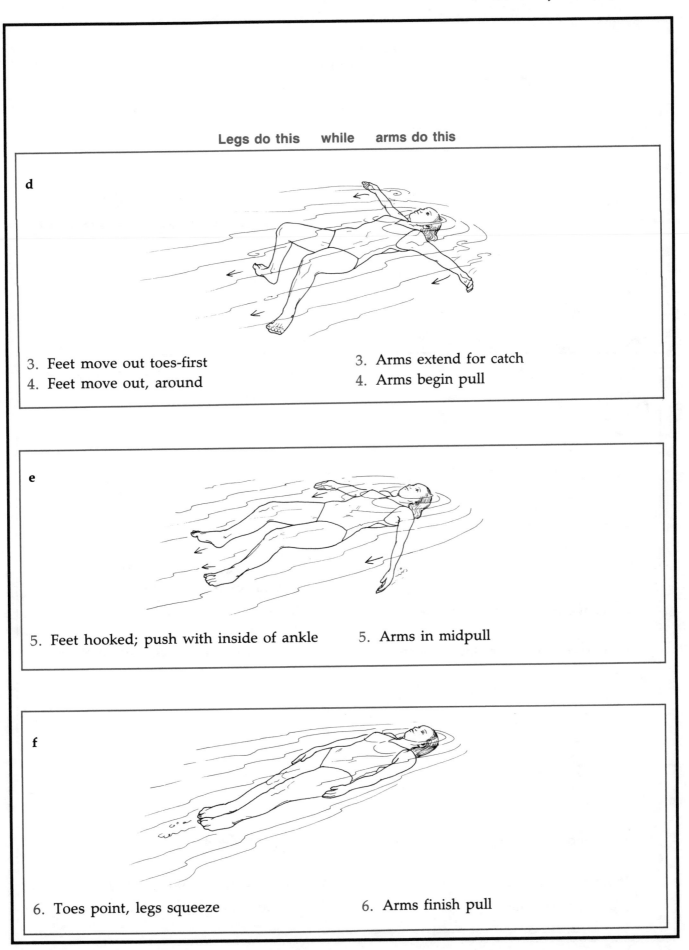

d

3. Feet move out toes-first

4. Feet move out, around

3. Arms extend for catch

4. Arms begin pull

e

5. Feet hooked; push with inside of ankle

5. Arms in midpull

f

6. Toes point, legs squeeze

6. Arms finish pull

Follow-Through Phase

1. Streamline, glide

Detecting Errors in Elementary Backstroke

Learning how to recognize a well-executed elementary backstroke is easier if you can compare correct and incorrect movements. The most common errors are listed below, with suggestions on how to correct them.

ERROR 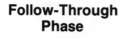 **CORRECTION**

ERROR	CORRECTION
1. Knees break surface.	1. Arch, do not bend at hips. Drop heels behind you.

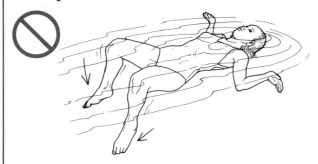

ERROR	CORRECTION
2. Water washes over face on recovery.	2. Recover slowly. *Sneak* hands up sides. Keep knees under. Lift chin.
3. Water washes over face on pull.	3. Tilt chin down slightly on pull. Pull levelly, not upward.
4. No power comes from kick.	4. *Hook* ankles; push using inside of foot, a wide kick, and a squeeze.
5. Arms and legs do not finish at same time.	5. Start pull slightly ahead of kick.
6. Rapid stroking exists.	6. Ride glide until motion slows.
7. Legs begin sinking.	7. You ride glide too long: stroke sooner.

Elementary Backstroke Drills

1. Elementary Backstroke Kick, Land Drill

Sit on the deck at the edge of the pool with your legs over the water to midthigh. Lean back on your arms. Hook your feet as far as you can and hold this position as you drop your heels behind you (a low pool deck will allow your feet to be in the water). Put your heels against the wall and turn your toes outward as far as you can. Keep your knees fairly close, but allow them to separate as far as they must to get your toes pointed outward. Simultaneously move your feet out, around, and together in half-circles, squeezing at the very last part of the movement. Keep your feet hooked and feel the push of the water on the inside of your ankles. Point your toes and streamline your legs at the end of the movement.

Success Goal = powerful backward thrust with inside of feet

Your Score = _____ your judgment: How strong is your kick?

2. Elementary Backstroke Kick Drill, Braced on Edge, Arms Wide

In shallow water, place your back against the pool wall. Reach back and outward to place your arms and elbows on the edge of the pool. Bend your hips 90 degrees at the waist, holding your feet out in front of you. With your knees about 4 inches apart, stay bent at the hips but also bend your knees and drop both heels toward the bottom of the pool, hooking your ankles as your feet drop. Keeping your ankles hooked, turn your toes outward as far as they will go. Catch the water with the inside of your feet as you push them in a circle—out, around, back, and together as your knees straighten. At the very last moment, point your toes and try to put the bottoms of your feet together, trying to prolong the kick with your toes and the bottom of your feet. It is important for your feet to move outward *before* your knees at the beginning of the kick.

Success Goal = 10 kicks in which you can feel water pressure on the inside of your feet, pushing you tighter against the wall

Your Score = (#) _____ kicks

3. Elementary Backstroke Kick Drill Against Pressure

Repeat Drill 2 with your friend or instructor standing in front of you, his or her hands against the insides of your feet, fingers under the arches, while you push around and back against the hands. *CAUTION—PRESS VERY LIGHTLY: THESE ARE WEAK MUSCLES!*

Success Goal = 3 kicks against very light resistance in which you get the feeling of backward pressure

Your Score = (#) _____ kicks

4. Elementary Backstroke Kick Drill, Kickboard on Chest

In shallow water, hold a kickboard fairly close to your chest. Float on your back, your hips elevated and straight. Keep your knees about 4 inches apart and drop your heels back under you as far as you can, with your feet fully hooked. Turn your toes outward, making sure your feet lead your knees as you kick out, around, back, and together with the sides of your feet. Kick with your legs separating widely, then squeezing together as you straighten your knees and point your toes at the end of the kick. Glide to a full stop.

Success Goal = 20 feet of headfirst progress

Your Score = (#) _____ feet

5. Whip Kick (Back), Kickboard on Chest

Repeat Drill 4 with emphasis on making the recovery (dropping your heels, turning out your toes) very slowly and the kick (whipping) quickly, with maximum glide in the streamlined position. Try for distance per kick.

Success Goal = 4 feet per kick average across the pool or 45 feet

Your Score = (#) _____ feet per kick

6. Coordinated Elementary Backstroke

Without a kickboard, float on your back, your arms outstretched. Drop your heels and prepare for a breaststroke kick. Begin a full arm pull, then deliver the kick. Try to finish pull and kick simultaneously. Glide until forward motion slows, then recover your arms by sliding your hands up along your sides. Simultaneously, begin to drop your heels behind you. As your hands turn out and start to reach up and out, turn your toes outward. Then pull and kick.

Success Goal = 10 full pulls and kicks ending simultaneously

Your Score = (#) _____ full pulls and kicks ending simultaneously

7. Elementary Backstroke, Distance per Stroke

Repeat Drill 6 with emphasis on distance traveled per stroke. Ride each glide for maximum distance, remaining streamlined but relaxed. Stretch for greater arm reach on the pull. Pull and kick with strength, then relax for rest.

Success Goal = 10 feet per stroke across the pool

Your Score = (#) _____ feet per stroke

8. Elementary Backstroke With Turn

In shallow water, push off the side wall on your back in back glide position. Begin a coordinated elementary backstroke. Near the other side, stop stroking with one arm and make a wide turn. Swim back to the start.

Success Goal = 2 pool widths, or 90 feet, with a smooth turn

Your Score = _____ your judgment: How smooth was your stroke and turn?

9. *Elementary Backstroke for Distance*

With your instructor watching, start at the shallow end of the pool. Push off the wall in a back glide position and swim a fully coordinated elementary backstroke to the deep end. Make a wide turn and swim back to the shallow end. Turn again and continue for a total of 4 pool lengths (with 3 turns).

Success Goal = 4 pool lengths, or 100 yards, and 3 turns

Your Score = (#) _____ yards and
(#) _____ turns

10. *Combination Crawl Stroke and Elementary Backstroke*

With your instructor watching, begin at the shallow end of the pool and swim the crawl stroke to the deep end. Make a wide turn and turn over onto your back. Swim the elementary backstroke back to the shallow end.

Success Goal = (qualitative) easy, rhythmic strokes; smooth turn and turnover

Your Score = _____ size of your smile as you realize how easy it was

Elementary Backstroke Keys to Success Checklist

As you progress, the evaluations become more and more qualitative in nature. You have just made some qualitative evaluations in the drills, but you need the opinion of an instructor as to the quality of your strokes. This checklist will help in the evaluation procedure.

**Preparation
Phase**

_____ An easy, relaxed back float with arms along side

Execution
Phase

Legs do this   while   arms do this

____ Heels drop down and back, feet fully hooked

____ Feet still hooked, toes turned out

____ Feet move outward, toes leading

____ Feet circle out, around

____ Feet hooked, pushing with inside of ankle

____ Toes point, legs squeeze

____ Arms recover, thumbs along sides

____ Hands turn, fingers point out from shoulders

____ Arms extend outward for "catch"

____ Arms begin pull

____ Arms pulling wide

____ Arms finish pull

**Follow-Through
Phase**

____ Body streamlined, relaxed; long glide

Step 17 **Breaststroke Pull**

The breaststroke pull is a rather short and somewhat ineffective pull that seems contrary to all our principles of long, full arm motions being best. It is necessary to keep this pull short and sharp, however, because of the way it coordinates with the kick to make a smooth, even stroke.

WHY IS THE BREASTSTROKE PULL IMPORTANT?

The breaststroke arm pull is important because it is the propulsive arm motion of a very important stroke. However, the breaststroke is a very kick-intensive stroke in which the kick provides more propulsion than the arm pull. The importance of the arm pull, then, is not so much in the propulsion it provides, but more as the basis and support for the kick that follows.

HOW TO EXECUTE THE BREASTSTROKE PULL

Start from a prone float, your arms extended. Flex your wrists, point your fingertips downward, and lift your elbows into the "over-the-barrel" position of the crawl stroke. Turn your hands to a slightly palm-out position. Lift your chin as you pull sharply in a semicircular

motion—out, back, and in—with your elbows bent 90 degrees and your fingertips pointing directly downward. Breathe as you finish the pull with your elbows out and your palms up under your chin. To recover, drop your face back into the water, bring your elbows in to your sides, but leave your hands at chin or neck level. Turn your hands palm-down and push them forward just under the water, fingertips leading, into full arm extension again. Normally a long glide would follow; however, with no kick to provide propulsion, your glide will be very short. Exhale on the glide.

ABOUT THE PULL

The pull should feel as if you were digging your fingertips into the water ahead and using them to pull your body through between them. Your elbows must remain as high as you can keep them until they are pulled in to the sides. Propulsion should come from the palms of your hands pulling outward and back, then inward and back to your chin. The entire pull is completed forward of your shoulders; your hands should never pull past shoulder level. Each hand moves approximately in a small half-circle from full extension to your chin. (see Figure 17.1).

*Figure 17.1 Keys to Success: **Breaststroke Pull***

Preparation Phase

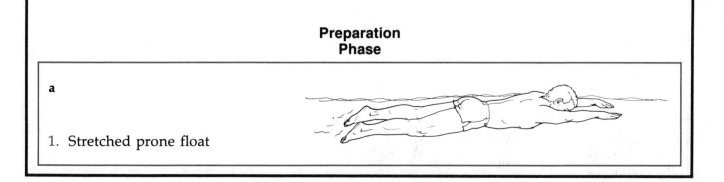

a

1. Stretched prone float

Execution Phase

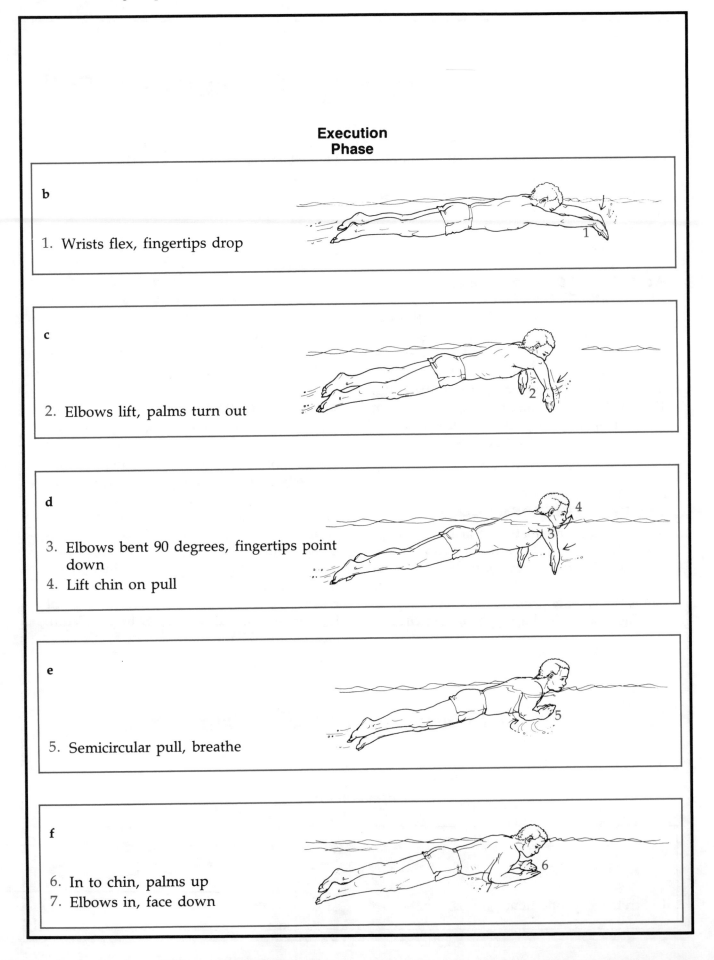

b

1. Wrists flex, fingertips drop

c

2. Elbows lift, palms turn out

d

3. Elbows bent 90 degrees, fingertips point down
4. Lift chin on pull

e

5. Semicircular pull, breathe

f

6. In to chin, palms up
7. Elbows in, face down

g

8. Extend arms, palms down

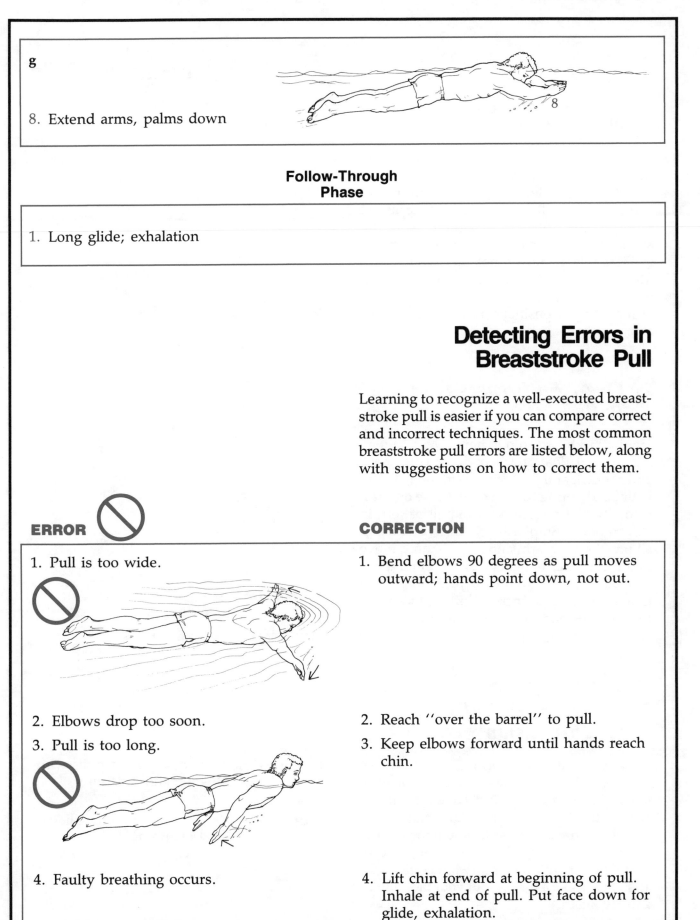

**Follow-Through
Phase**

1. Long glide; exhalation

Detecting Errors in Breaststroke Pull

Learning to recognize a well-executed breaststroke pull is easier if you can compare correct and incorrect techniques. The most common breaststroke pull errors are listed below, along with suggestions on how to correct them.

ERROR 🚫

CORRECTION

1. Pull is too wide.

1. Bend elbows 90 degrees as pull moves outward; hands point down, not out.

2. Elbows drop too soon.

2. Reach "over the barrel" to pull.

3. Pull is too long.

3. Keep elbows forward until hands reach chin.

4. Faulty breathing occurs.

4. Lift chin forward at beginning of pull. Inhale at end of pull. Put face down for glide, exhalation.

Breaststroke Pull Drills

1. Slow Motion Breaststroke Pulls

In shallow water, attach a deep float leg support to one ankle. Put on your mask and snorkel; this will allow you to concentrate more on the arm stroke without worrying about breathing. Practice stroking as described in Figure 17.1, but do not raise your head. Move your arms in very slow motion without thought of propulsion. Concentrate on correct arm and hand positions as you float.

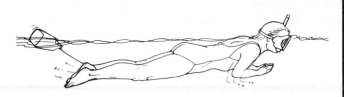

Success Goal = 20 correctly executed, slow-motion arm strokes while floating

Your Score = (#) _____ arm strokes

2. One-Arm Breaststroke Pulls

Hold a kickboard in one hand. With a deep leg support float attached, wear your mask and snorkel, and float face down; do not raise your head during this exercise. Move one arm through the breaststroke arm pull pattern in slow motion. Emphasize the high elbow position. Your forearm and hand should move in a semicircle, hanging down from a high, bent elbow. Keep your palm facing the direction of motion as it circles. Shift the kickboard to the other hand and work with the opposite arm.

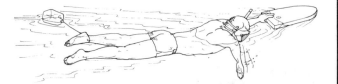

Success Goal = 30 practice pulls with each arm

Your Score = (#) _____ pulls

3. Breaststroke Pulls for Propulsion

Using a leg support float, but without mask and snorkel, change the emphasis of practice pulls to gaining propulsion. Digging in forcefully with your fingertips, pull sharply and quickly with your forearms and hands to the position under your chin. Bring your elbows in and thrust your hands forward easily. Stop and glide. Take a breath, put your face down, and try again.

Success Goal = 40 quick, hard pulls with glide and breathing between

Your Score = (#) _____ pulls with glide and breathing

4. Coordinated Breaststroke Breathing

Repeat Drill 3, but start by exhaling before the first pull. Then, using the pull of your hands to help, lift your chin forward until it is at water level. Open your mouth and inhale as your hands pull inward to your chin. At the end of the pull, while your elbows are squeezing inward, drop your face back into the water. Thrust your arms forward; exhale on the glide. Be ready to lift your chin again on the next pull. Be careful not to press down on the water more than is absolutely necessary to thrust your chin forward. Keeping your elbows high helps keep the pull in the right direction.

Success Goal = 20 consecutive pulls with successful breathing

Your Score = (#) _____ pulls

5. Breaststroke Pull, Pool Width

With a leg float attached, pull and breathe for distance and comfortable breathing. Keep the pull short and quick, the recovery slow and easy. Do not pull your hands past your shoulders.

Success Goal = one pool width, or 45 feet, pulling and breathing

Your Score = (#) _____ feet pulling and breathing

6. Breaststroke Pulls in Deep Water

With your instructor watching and with a leg float attached, start at the deep end of the pool with a prone glide. Pull and breathe to the shallow end.

Success Goal = one pool length or 75 feet

Your Score = (#) _____ feet

Breaststroke Pull
Keys to Success Checklist

You have met several quantitative goals. How *well* you do the breaststroke pulls is really more important than how far, though. Ask your teacher, coach, or a trained observer to evaluate your technique qualitatively according to the checklist below. He or she may decide you need more work on one aspect or another before you should continue.

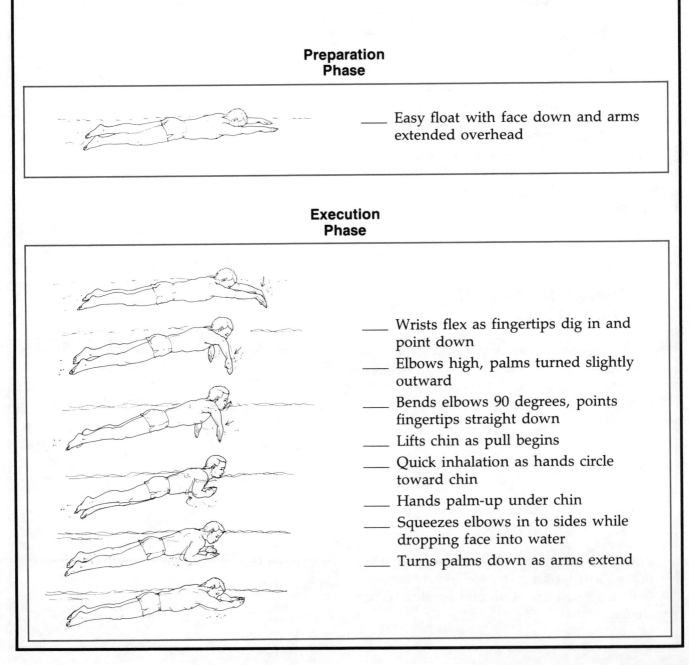

**Preparation
Phase**

_____ Easy float with face down and arms extended overhead

**Execution
Phase**

_____ Wrists flex as fingertips dig in and point down

_____ Elbows high, palms turned slightly outward

_____ Bends elbows 90 degrees, points fingertips straight down

_____ Lifts chin as pull begins

_____ Quick inhalation as hands circle toward chin

_____ Hands palm-up under chin

_____ Squeezes elbows in to sides while dropping face into water

_____ Turns palms down as arms extend

**Follow-Through
Phase**

_____ Exhales on the long glide

Step 18 **Breaststroke**

The breaststroke is selected more than any other stroke for easy, comfortable swimming in the prone position. When properly swum, it requires rhythmic breathing with your face submerged during the glide. However, it adapts very easily to a semivertical position with your head held up to see and to converse with other swimmers. It is, therefore, often called the "social" or "conversational" stroke. It is not a fast stroke, but it is the most comfortable for long distances.

The breaststroke is used in competition; when so swum, it is subject to more restricting and qualifying rules than any other stroke. Because of this, there are more definite "right" and "wrong" ways to swim this stroke than any other.

WHY IS THE BREASTSTROKE IMPORTANT?

The breaststroke is a lifesaving stroke. It requires very little energy, because your arms are recovered underwater and natural flotation keeps you afloat. When swimming a long distance is necessary, the ease with which it is swum becomes a lifesaving factor. You have learned that you can rest by turning over onto your back to keep your face free of the water. In choppy waves, sometimes the back position is not the most comfortable. The breaststroke offers an alternative and permits you to see where you are going at the same time. This stroke provides the easiest method for keeping your head up while in a prone position.

HOW TO SWIM THE BREASTSTROKE

You have already learned the breaststroke kick, but only on your back. If you turn the breaststroke kick over and add the breaststroke arm pull with proper timing and coordination, the breaststroke will be easy.

From a prone float position, start the breaststroke arm pull and head lift. While pulling and lifting your head, bring both heels up behind you in the breaststroke kick recovery. Inhale quickly. As your hands rotate during the elbow squeeze, your feet should be rotating outward in preparation for the leg thrust. Drop your face down into the water as you thrust your hands forward and kick vigorously. Streamline your body and take a long glide as you exhale (see Figure 18.1).

Figure 18.1 Keys to Success: Breaststroke

Preparation Phase

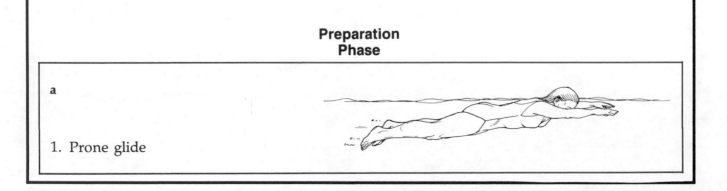

a

1. Prone glide

**Execution
Phase**

b

1. Pull, raise head; heels up
2. Feet hooked, turned out

c

3. Hands under chin; feet move out

d

4. Head drops, legs thrust, arms extend

**Follow-Through
Phase**

1. Long glide; exhalation

Detecting Errors in the Breaststroke

Learning to recognize a well-executed breast-stroke is easier if you can compare correct and incorrect techniques. The most common breast-stroke errors are listed below, along with suggestions on how to correct them.

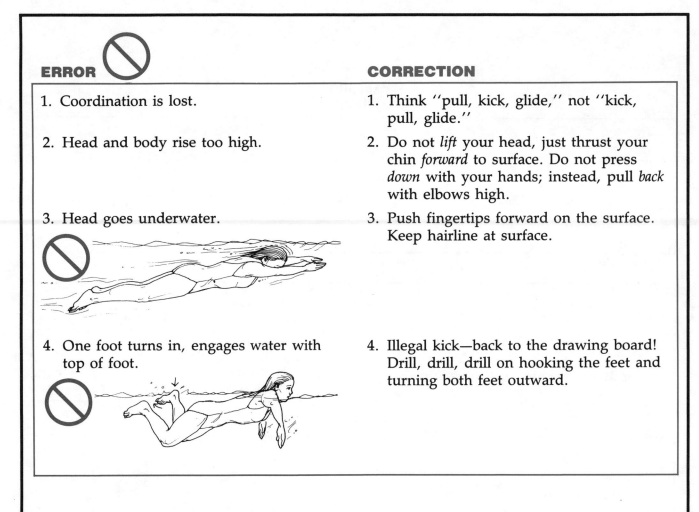

ERROR 🚫

CORRECTION

1. Coordination is lost.

2. Head and body rise too high.

3. Head goes underwater.

4. One foot turns in, engages water with top of foot.

1. Think "pull, kick, glide," not "kick, pull, glide."

2. Do not *lift* your head, just thrust your chin *forward* to surface. Do not press *down* with your hands; instead, pull *back* with elbows high.

3. Push fingertips forward on the surface. Keep hairline at surface.

4. Illegal kick—back to the drawing board! Drill, drill, drill on hooking the feet and turning both feet outward.

Breaststroke Drills

1. Breaststroke Kick, Bracket Drill

Review the breaststroke kick in the elementary backstroke position. Then turn over and grasp the pool edge with one hand and position the other hand directly below, palm against the wall and fingers pointing to the bottom of the pool. By pulling on the top hand and pushing with the lower hand (gently), you can hold a position with your feet near the surface. If your body swings to one side, move your bottom hand slightly toward that side. When comfortable in this "bracket" position, bring both heels up behind you in the breaststroke kick recovery. Do not hold your feet so close to the surface that your heels come out

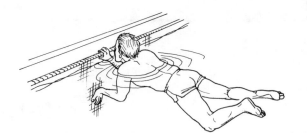

of the water. Allow your legs to sink far enough to keep your heels under. Practice the breaststroke kick in the bracket position, concentrating on the backward thrust with the inside of your ankles.

Success Goal = feeling the thrust of your feet driving you against the wall

Your Score = _____ thrust felt (yes or no?)

2. Breaststroke Kick Against Resistance

Repeat Drill 1 with someone standing behind you, placing their hands on the insides of your ankles and their fingers curling up over the soles of your feet as you kick against the resistance they provide. *CAUTION!* DO NOT PUSH VERY HARD. THESE ARE WEAK MUSCLES.

Success Goal = experiencing how the pressure should feel when you kick

Your Score = _____ pressure felt (yes or no)?

3. Breaststroke Kick With Kickboard

Holding a kickboard at arm's length with both hands, practice the breaststroke kick for propulsion. Keep your chin as low as possible to breathe. Do not bring your knees in under your body on the recovery. Bring your heels up behind you. Your hips should not bend very much.

Success Goal = one pool width or 45 feet

Your Score = (#) _____ feet

4. Breaststroke Coordination With Mask, Snorkel

Float on the surface face down with mask and snorkel. With absolutely no thought about propulsion, work on the coordination between your arms and legs. Start lifting your heels as the pull begins. Hook your feet and point your toes out as the pull finishes. Your feet move outward while your elbows squeeze in to your sides; your legs thrust as your arms extend palm down. Do this drill in *very slow motion* while floating.

Success Goal = 40 slow-motion strokes

Your Score = (#) _____ slow-motion strokes

5. Breaststroke Coordination Without Mask, Snorkel

Repeat Drill 4 without the mask and snorkel. Hold your breath and keep your face down during the pull and kick. Exhale and take a new breath by raising your chin during the glide phase, then keep your face underwater for the next stroke. Move *very* slowly. Do not try to move forward.

Success Goal = 40 slow-motion strokes

Your Score = (#) _____ slow-motion strokes

6. Coordinating Breaststroke With Breathing

Begin with a stretched prone float. Exhale and begin to raise your head on the first stroke. Pull for propulsion and inhale during the stroke. Drop your head back into the water as your hands come in under your chin. Exhale after the leg thrust, as you glide in a stretched position. Do one stroke at a time. Ride your glide while you concentrate on the beginning movements of the next stroke.

Success Goal = 20 strokes with easily coordinated breathing

Your Score = (#) _____ strokes

7. Breaststroke Distance per Stroke

Swim the breaststroke with emphasis on the length of the glide. Try to cross the pool in 2 or 3 strokes by pulling and thrusting with power and by stretching the glide.

Success Goal = 4 strokes for a 45 foot pool, or an average of over 10 feet per stroke

Your Score = (#) _____ average feet per stroke

8. Breaststroke in Deep Water

With your instructor watching, start at the deep end of the pool. Push off in a prone glide and swim a fully coordinated breaststroke to the shallow end of the pool, or 45 feet.

Success Goal = at least 25 feet in deep water

Your Score = (#) _____ feet

9. *Breaststroke for Distance*

With your instructor watching, start at the shallow end of the pool. Swim the breaststroke to the deep end of the pool. Grasp the edge of the pool, tuck your legs, and turn your body. Place your feet against the wall and push off. Hold your glide for 3 seconds before resuming the breaststroke. Swim to the shallow end and repeat the wall turn. Continue swimming until you have swum 100 yards.

Success Goal = 100 yards

Your Score = (#) _____ yards

10. *Breaststroke Adaptation*

Swim the breaststroke with your head above water, your chin constantly at water level. Allow your feet and legs to drop into a semivertical position and do not try to glide at all. Constantly alternate leg kicks and arm strokes to keep you up but do not try to rise above chin level. Breathe whenever you wish. Make forward progress slowly, if at all. This "conversational" adaptation of the breaststroke is one of its nicest features.

Success Goal = 5 minutes in the semivertical mode with comfort

Your Score = (#) _____ minutes

Breaststroke
Keys to Success Checklist

It is important to swim for distance, but a qualitative judgment of how well you swim the stroke is also important. Someone who knows the stroke well should watch you swim and evaluate you according to the checklist below.

**Preparation
Phase**

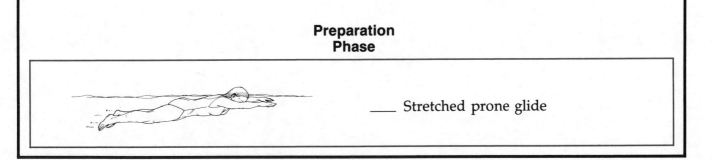

_____ Stretched prone glide

Execution
Phase

___ Head lifts early in pull as heels come up

___ Feet are hooked; toes, pointed out

___ Feet move out as hands come in under the chin

___ Face drops into water as the legs thrust and the arms extend

Follow-Through
Phase

___ Long glide during exhalation

Step 19 Scissors Kick

The scissors kick is used in the sidestroke. It is performed in the side glide position. Because the side glide is already familiar to you, you should have no trouble learning the scissors kick.

WHY IS THE SCISSORS KICK IMPORTANT?

The scissors kick is the most powerful kick known. It is used in lifesaving because it provides the power necessary to tow a drowning victim. It provides a longer glide and rest than any other kick, and is easier than the breaststroke kick because it uses the forward-back motion that we use every day in walking. It is important as the workhorse of all the kicks.

HOW TO EXECUTE A SCISSORS KICK

Hold a kickboard under one ear like a violin. Starting in a side glide position, bend at your knees and hips to bring both feet in a direct line toward your body. When your knees are fully bent (hips at 90 degrees), hook your top foot and step out forward as if to step up onto a high step. At the same time, point the toes of your lower foot and step back as far as you can, as if to lay your toes on top of a large step behind you. Now step forward *and back* as far as you can as the legs thrust and squeeze back together, straightening to full extension. Point the toes of both feet during the thrust. Finish with your feet together and streamlined. Turn your toes in slightly so they catch on each other at the finish (see Figure 19.1). G-l-i-d-e!

Figure 19.1 Keys to Success: *Scissors Kick*

Preparation Phase

a

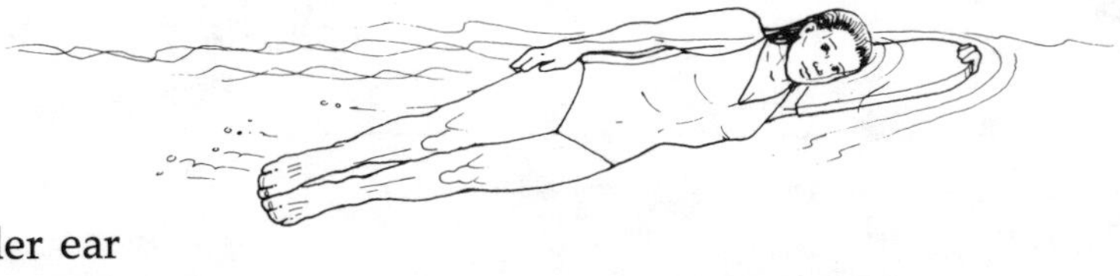

1. Side glide position, kickboard under ear

**Execution
Phase**

b

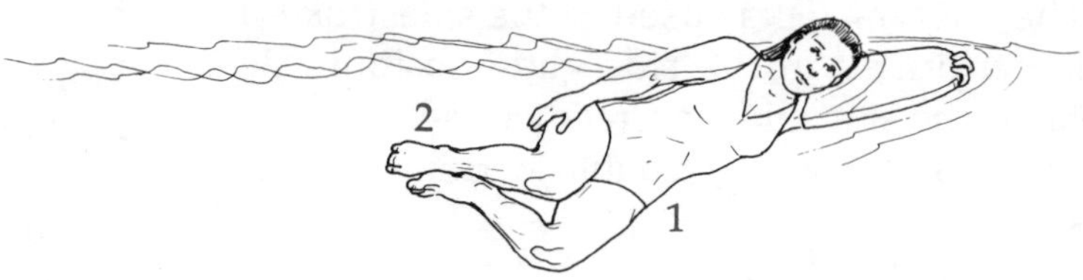

1. Legs tuck, hips 90 degrees
2. Feet in line with body

c

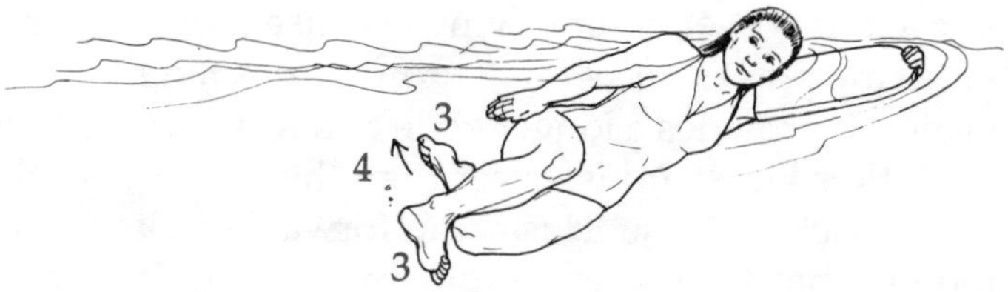

3. Top foot hooks, lower foot points
4. Top foot forward, lower foot back

d

5. Step wide, drive, squeeze
6. Toes point, streamline body

**Follow-Through
Phase**

1. Long glide

Detecting Errors in Scissors Kick

Learning to recognize a well-executed scissors kick is easier if you can compare correct and incorrect techniques. The most common scissors kick errors are listed below, along with suggestions to correct them.

ERROR

CORRECTION

1. Feet are forward of body in tuck position.

1. Bend only 90 degrees at hips; knees bend more.

2. Lower thigh still points forward after stepping out.

2. Step back farther with lower leg.

3. Stepping out rolls you onto stomach.

3. Consciously roll hips back.

4. Thrust is straight back.

4. Step *out*, around, and thrust.

5. Feet pass each other.

5. Turn feet inward to cross and catch.

Scissors Kick Drills

1. Scissors Kick, Land Drill

Lie on your side on a mat, one arm stretched forward under your ear, the other along your side. Bring your knees up but keep your feet back in line with your body. Check the position of your feet. Point the toes of your lower foot and hook your upper foot at the ankle. Step out forward with your top foot and backward with your bottom leg in as big a step as possible without rolling your hips forward. Stop and check to see whether your lower leg is as far back as it will go (lower thigh straight with body). Then carefully move your feet *out*, around, and down together in a circular motion. Streamline your legs and toes for a glide.

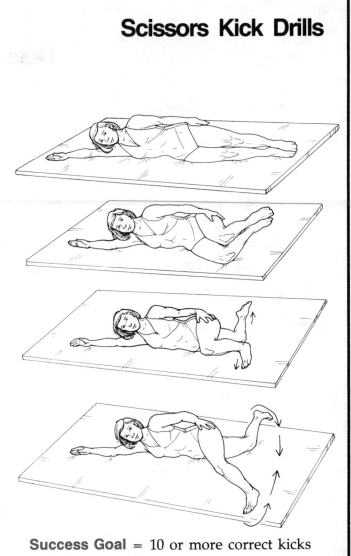

Success Goal = 10 or more correct kicks

Your Score = (#) _____ kicks

2. Scissors Kick, Bracket Drill

In shallow water at the side of the pool, turn your side to the wall. Lay your cheek on the water with the top of your head toward the wall. With your top hand, grasp the pool edge. Place your bottom hand against the pool wall about 18 inches deep, with your palm against the wall and fingertips pointing down (bracket position). Your lower hand must be directly under your top hand. Now pull slightly with your top hand and push slightly with your bottom hand to bring your feet off the bottom

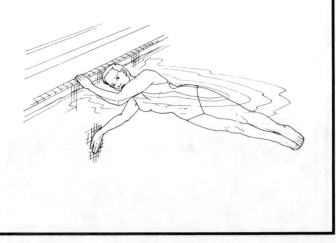

in a side float position. If your body moves to the side, move your bottom hand slightly in the same direction until you can hold the side position comfortably. Keep your ear underwater. Recover your legs slowly as in the land drill, hook the top foot, point the lower foot, and step out *slowly* (top foot forward, bottom foot back). Then drive out, around, and down with vigor. Stop in the glide position. Do not let your feet pass each other.

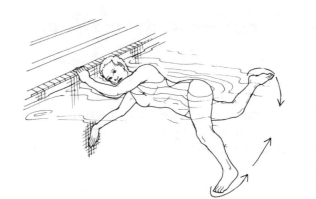

Success Goal = 30 bracket drill kicks

Your Score = (#) _____ bracket drill kicks

3. Scissors Kick With Kickboard

Take a side float position, your lower arm extended under your head and your upper arm along your side. Hold a kickboard lengthwise under your upper arm and fairly close to your hip. Use the scissors kick across the pool.

Success Goal = one pool width or 45 feet kicking and gliding

Your Score = (#) _____ feet

4. Distance per Scissors Kick

In a side glide position, hold a kickboard lengthwise in your forward arm (under your head) like a violin. Keep your ear pressed tightly to the board. Grasp the lower corner of the kickboard with the fingertips of your other hand. Push off the bottom into a side glide and begin the scissors kick. Make the kick as wide as you can and try for distance on the glide. Remember to balance on your side for the glide by bending slightly at your hips to prevent rolling onto your back; arch slightly to prevent rolling onto your stomach. Kick across the pool.

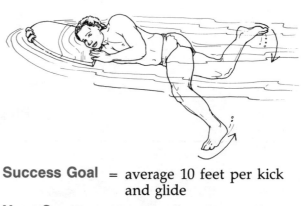

Success Goal = average 10 feet per kick and glide

Your Score = (#) _____ feet (average)

5. *Scissors Kick for Distance*

Using a kickboard as you wish—either under your ear or on your top hip—kick across the pool. Turn immediately, push off, and kick back again. Continue without stopping to rest on the turns until you have completed 4 pool widths or 180 feet. Stay in shallow water.

Success Goal = 4 pool widths or 180 feet without rest

Your Score = (#) _____ feet

6. *Scissors Kick and Top Hand Push*

Hold a kickboard like a violin, but place your other hand on the front of the thigh of your top leg. As your legs recover for the scissors kick, allow your top hand to remain on the front of your thigh, your elbow bending as necessary. During the thrust of your legs, push with your hand on the front of your thigh as if to help your leg push against the water. This is the first step in a progression to coordinate the sidestroke arm motion with the scissors kick.

Success Goal = 40 kicks with glide while pushing on thigh

Your Score = (#) _____ kicks

Scissors Kick
Keys to Success Checklist

Rhythm and efficiency are hard to measure quantitatively in a swimming stroke. However, they are important, so have your coach or teacher evaluate your scissors kick qualitatively using this checklist. These points may indicate areas where more practice is needed.

**Preparation
Phase**

_____ Side glide with kickboard held in violin position

Execution
Phase

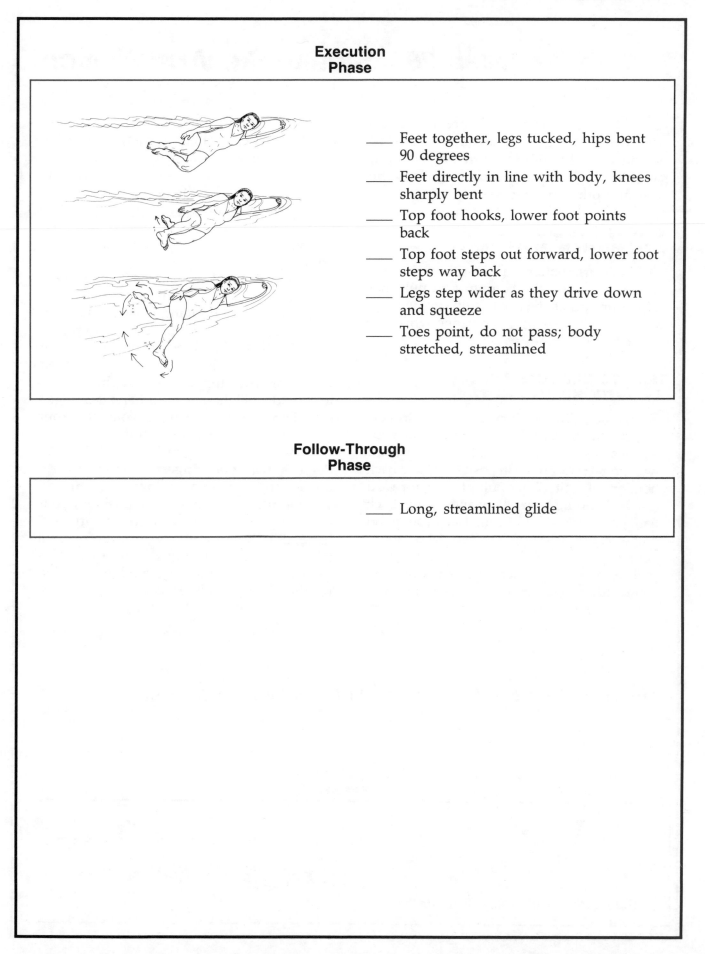

___ Feet together, legs tucked, hips bent 90 degrees

___ Feet directly in line with body, knees sharply bent

___ Top foot hooks, lower foot points back

___ Top foot steps out forward, lower foot steps way back

___ Legs step wider as they drive down and squeeze

___ Toes point, do not pass; body stretched, streamlined

Follow-Through
Phase

___ Long, streamlined glide

Step 20 Sidestroke Arm Motion

The arms move in opposite directions in the sidestroke. The upper, rearward arm pushes simultaneously with the thrust of the kick, whereas the lower, forward arm pulls as the legs and other arm recover.

WHY IS THE SIDESTROKE ARM MOTION IMPORTANT?

Only one arm pattern fits the sidestroke. It is unique in that it is the only arm pull that allows one arm to be free to stop stroking and hold onto something or someone while the other arm continues its pull.

HOW TO EXECUTE THE SIDESTROKE ARM MOTION

From a side glide position, your lower arm extended forward under your head and your upper arm along your side, flex your forward wrist to put your hand in position to pull back horizontally. Start the pull of your forward arm by bending your elbow and pulling back with your hand and forearm. Allow your hand and forearm to assume a horizontal position, your elbow bent 90 degrees, as you begin to pull from your shoulder. Pull as though you were gathering an armful of water and pulling it in to your chest. When your forward

elbow is pointing straight down, bring your hand up under your ear, turning it palm-up. Squeeze your elbow to your side, point your fingertips forward, and fully extend your arm palm-up just under the surface. Turn your palm down as it reaches full extension. Glide until ready for the next stroke. Your upper, rearward arm moves opposite your forward arm.

As your forward arm begins its pull, press the elbow of your other arm into your side; bend the elbow, bringing your top hand to your chin. Leave your palm down; keep your hand flat under the water as it moves. As your forward hand is turning palm-up under your lower ear, your top arm is brought forward to shoulder height, and your hand is plunged deep into the water in front of your face. Your top arm is now extended straight out from your shoulder, and your elbow is bent 90 degrees, with your fingers pointing straight down at the bottom of the pool. As your forward arm extends to starting position, your top arm pushes water, with the forearm and hand, directly backward toward your feet until it rests once again along your side. This returns your body to a streamlined position for the glide (see Figure 20.1).

Figure 20.1 Keys to Success: *Sidestroke Arm Motion*

**Preparation
Phase**

a

1. Side glide position (leg float attached)

Execution
Phase

Rearward (upper) arm does this   while   forward (lower) arm does this

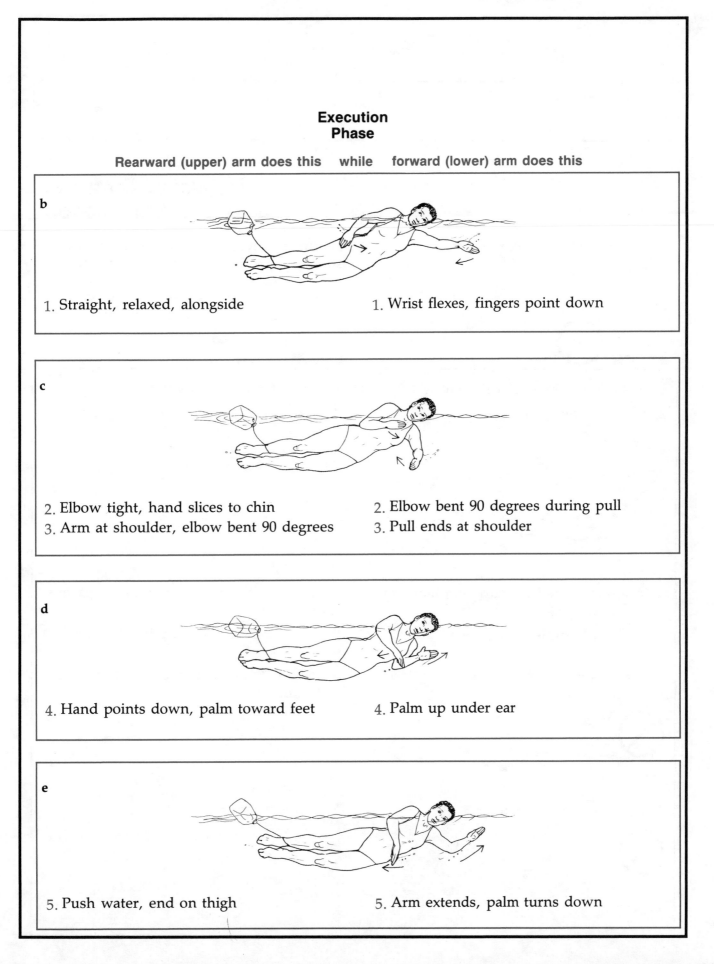

b

1. Straight, relaxed, alongside

1. Wrist flexes, fingers point down

c

2. Elbow tight, hand slices to chin
3. Arm at shoulder, elbow bent 90 degrees

2. Elbow bent 90 degrees during pull
3. Pull ends at shoulder

d

4. Hand points down, palm toward feet

4. Palm up under ear

e

5. Push water, end on thigh

5. Arm extends, palm turns down

**Follow-Through
Phase**

1. G-l-i-d-e

Detecting Errors in Sidestroke Arm Motion

Learning to recognize a well-executed side-stroke arm motion is easier if you can compare correct and incorrect techniques. The most common sidestroke errors are listed below, along with suggestions for correcting them.

ERROR

CORRECTION

ERROR	CORRECTION
1. Forward arm pulls out in front.	1. Pull *down* with elbow bent.
2. Forward arm pulls too far.	2. Don't pull past shoulder; bring hand up to ear.
3. Head is lifted on pull.	3. Keep ear underwater.

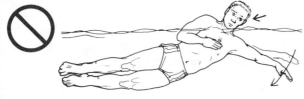

4. Water is pushed forward with hand on extension.	4. Keep wrist straight, hand flat, fingertips first.
5. Rearward arm is out of water.	5. Press elbow to side, dig hand in deep for push.
6. Water is pushed on recovery with top hand.	6. Palm flat and wrist straight, slice hand through water.

7. Top hand reaches too far.	7. Dig hand in at chin.

Sidestroke Arm Motion Drills

1. Sidestroke Forward Arm Pull, With Support

Assume a side glide position with a deep leg float support attached to your upper ankle. Hold a kickboard under your upper arm, keeping it fairly close to your armpit to support your upper body. Keep your ear on the water and start to pull with your forward arm as described above. Pull in very slow motion as you float, so you can study your arm motion. Do not try for propulsion or distance at first. As you become accustomed to the motion, make the pull rather quickly and sneak your hand forward again, slowly, with the least possible resistance. Stop in the glide position but do not expect to glide very far. Inhale as you pull and exhale as you glide.

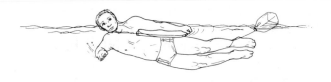

Success Goal = 40 pulls with breathing

Your Score = (#) _____ forward arm pulls

2. Sidestroke Upper Arm Push, With Support

Using a deep leg support and holding a kickboard under your ear like a violin, assume a side float position. Start the motion by recovering your upper hand from its position on your thigh. Keep your hand flat on the water, your wrist straight. Leave your elbow close to your side as it bends, bringing your hand to your chin. As you dig downward into the water with your hand, allow your elbow to move forward until it is straight out in front of your shoulder. Keep a 90-degree bend in your elbow, your fingertips pointing directly to the bottom of the pool. Now push water toward your feet with your forearm and hand until your arm is straight and resting on your thigh again. Inhale on the recovery and exhale on the glide.

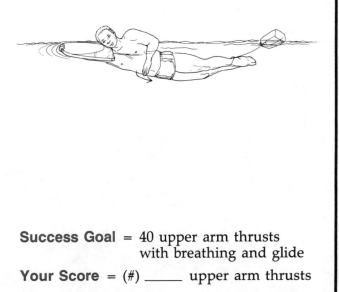

Success Goal = 40 upper arm thrusts with breathing and glide

Your Score = (#) _____ upper arm thrusts

3. Coordinated Sidestroke Arm Pull, Feet Supported

Use a deep leg support float, but no kickboard. Start in the side glide position. Pull with your forward arm as your top arm recovers, then push with your top arm as your forward arm recovers. Think about it as though you were gathering an armful of water ahead of you, bringing it back to your chest, then transferring the same water to your other hand to push it on toward your feet. As you begin to use both arms efficiently, you will begin to get some forward motion. Do not expect a lot of propulsion, but ride each glide as far as you can.

Success Goal = one pool width or 45 feet of forward motion

Your Score = (#) _____ feet

Sidestroke Arm Motion Keys to Success Checklist

Distance is a quantitative method for determining progress. However, it does not address the ease and fluidity with which you stroke. Have your instructor use the following checklist to evaluate your technique qualitatively and to make suggestions for improvement.

Preparation Phase

_____ Side glide position with leg float attached

Execution
Phase

Rearward (upper) arm does this   while   **forward (lower) arm does this**

____ Remains straight and relaxed, hand resting on thigh

____ Elbow tight to side as hand slices to chin

____ Arm moves to shoulder height, elbow bent 90 degrees

____ Hand and forearm straight down, palm turned toward feet

____ Push water straight back; hand ends on thigh

____ Wrist flexes, fingertips point toward bottom

____ Elbow bends 90 degrees as hand and forearm pull

____ Pull ends at shoulder, elbow points down

____ Elbow close to side, hand palm-up under ear

____ Arm extends forward, palm turns down

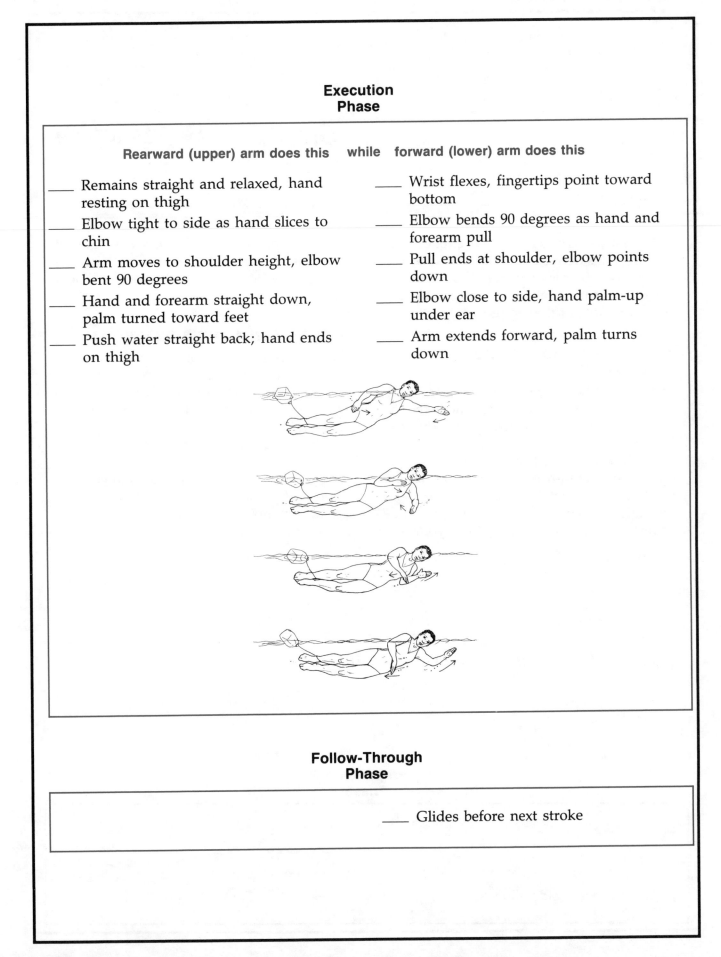

Follow-Through
Phase

____ Glides before next stroke

Step 21 Sidestroke

The sidestroke is a kick-intensive stroke: Most of its power is derived from the kick. One arm aids the kick in providing propulsion, whereas the other arm simply compensates for the negative effect of the leg recovery.

WHY IS THE SIDESTROKE IMPORTANT?

The sidestroke employs the scissors kick, which is so powerful that it does not need the added propulsion provided by the top arm. This means that one arm can be free to do other things. Rather heavy objects or people can be carried or towed simply by shortening the glide somewhat. If you choose to use both arms, this stroke allows you the longest glide or rest period of any stroke. Also, your face is always above water, so you may breathe at any time you wish. For swimming long distances, the sidestroke is the most efficient stroke.

HOW TO SWIM THE SIDESTROKE

From a side glide position, pull with your forward arm as your legs and top arm recover. Thrust with the scissors kick and push with your top arm as your forward arm recovers. The kick coincides with the forward thrust of the forward arm, ending the stroke with power and in the streamlined position for a long glide. It seems almost as though your top hand and your legs were tied together, because they move in the same direction at the same time (see Figure 21.1).

Figure 21.1 Keys to Success: Sidestroke

Preparation Phase

a

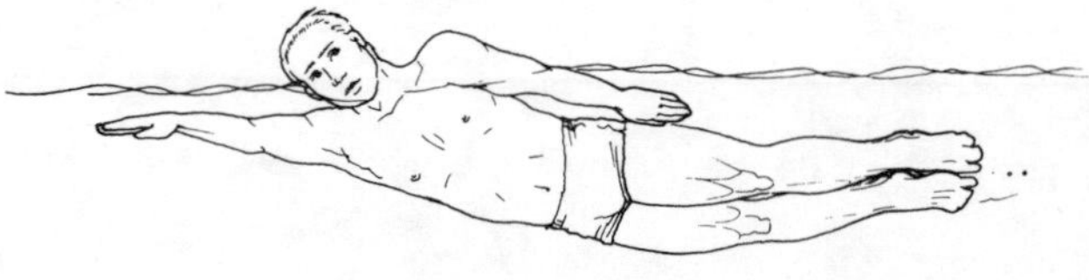

1. Easy, relaxed, side glide

Execution
Phase

Forward arm does this   while   legs and top arm do this

b

1. Pull to shoulder, inhale, palm under ear

1. Knees drawn up, top hand to chin

c

2. Forward elbow in, fingers point forward
3. Forward arm extends palm-down

2. Feet step out, hand digs in
3. Strong leg kick, top arm push

Follow-Through
Phase

d

1. Long glide; exhalation

Detecting Errors in the Sidestroke

The most common errors in the sidestroke are errors in kick or arm motion. Both of these categories have been covered in Steps 19 and 20. In the present step, coordination between kick and arm stroke is most important. If the top arm works with the legs and the forward arm opposes the kick, there is very seldom a coordination error.

ERROR 	CORRECTION
1. Head tilts up.	1. Keep ear underwater.
2. Forward arm pulls too far.	2. Forward arm must always stop at shoulder height.
3. Top hand pulls out too far.	3. Top forearm should point straight down, 6 inches from body.
4. Top hand enters too low.	4. Top hand should dig in at about eyebrow level.
5. You move diagonally or in a long curve.	5. Lower leg needs to step back farther.

Sidestroke Coordination Drills

1. Top Arm–Kick Coordination With Kickboard

Hold a kickboard at arm's length with your forward hand. Lay your top hand on the front of the thigh of your top leg. Kick, using the scissors kick. Allow your elbow to bend as your legs are recovered, but keep your hand on your leg. During the thrust of the kick, press on your thigh with your hand as if to help it kick. After the third or fourth kick, gradually remove your hand from your thigh, but continue to make the same movement pattern with your hand 3 to 5 inches forward of your thigh. Keep the same coordination between hand and leg, but move your hand farther forward on each stroke until your hand is slicing to your chin and digging in to push on the water in correct sidestroke motion.

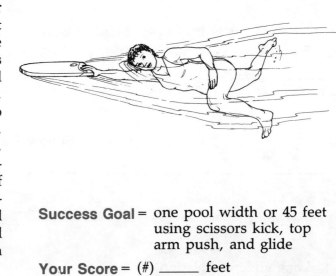

Success Goal = one pool width or 45 feet using scissors kick, top arm push, and glide

Your Score = (#) _____ feet

2. Forward Arm– Kick Coordination With Kickboard

In sidestroke position, hold a kickboard under your top arm and near your top hip. From a glide position, pull with your forward arm and recover your legs for a scissors kick. Stop momentarily when your feet are ready to step out and your hand is under your ear. Check that everything is ready for a leg thrust and simultaneous arm extension to glide position. Then kick and reach into a long glide. Continue to hesitate at this coordination checkpoint for a few strokes, then eliminate the hesitation and swim the stroke smoothly with a long glide.

Success Goal = 40 properly coordinated forward-arm pulls and scissors kicks, smooth and coordinated

Your Score = (#) _____ pulls and kicks

3. Fully Coordinated Sidestroke

In shallow water, push off from the side and swim a fully coordinated sidestroke across the pool. Turn, push off, and swim back again. Continue to swim widths, concentrating on timing, smoothness, and distance per stroke.

Success Goal = 6 widths continuously

Your Score = (#) _____ widths

4. Sidestroke Distance per Stroke

Push off the side wall and swim a fully coordinated sidestroke across the pool. Count your strokes. Try for an average of 6 feet or more per stroke.

Success Goal = 6 feet per stroke

Your Score = (#) _____ feet per stroke

5. Deep-Water Sidestroke

With your instructor watching, start at the deep end of the pool. Push off and swim to the shallow end. Count your strokes. Try to average 6 feet or more per stroke.

Success Goal = 75 feet in 12 strokes, or over 6 feet per stroke

Your Score = (#) _____ feet per stroke

6. 2 Lengths Sidestroke

With your instructor watching, push off from the shallow end of the pool and swim to the deep end. Immediately push off from the deep end and swim back to the shallow end. Concentrate on smoothness and relaxation.

Success Goal = 2 lengths or 150 feet

Your Score = (#) _____ feet

7. 100 Yards Sidestroke

Swim a smooth and coordinated sidestroke, inhaling on the forward arm pull and exhaling on the glide.

Success Goal = 4 pool lengths or 100 yards, turning and pushing off at each end of the pool

Your Score = (#) _____ yards

8. Lifesaving Sidestroke

Swim the sidestroke across the pool, using only your legs and forward arm. Your top arm is used to hold a 10-pound diving brick or similar weight item on your top hip. Do not try to glide, but alternate stroking and kicking continuously.

Success Goal = one pool width or 45 feet carrying 10 pounds

Your Score = (#) _____ feet

Sidestroke
Keys to Success Checklist

This particular stroke lends itself to the quantitative measurement of power because weight is carried a distance. This still doesn't give you a measure of confidence, relaxation, or feeling of fluid dynamics, which can only be assessed qualitatively. Ask your teacher to evaluate your stroke qualitatively with the help of the checklist below.

**Preparation
Phase**

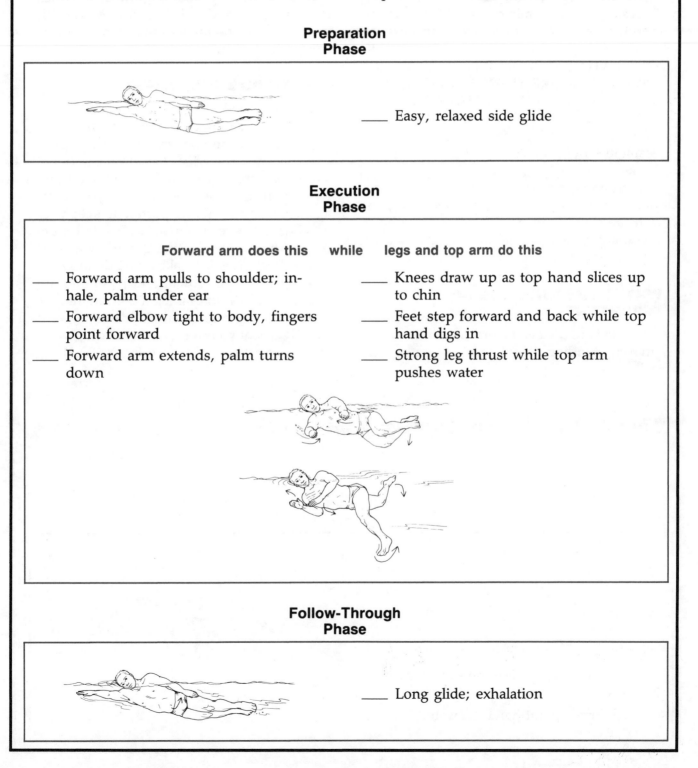

____ Easy, relaxed side glide

**Execution
Phase**

Forward arm does this   while   legs and top arm do this

____ Forward arm pulls to shoulder; inhale, palm under ear

____ Forward elbow tight to body, fingers point forward

____ Forward arm extends, palm turns down

____ Knees draw up as top hand slices up to chin

____ Feet step forward and back while top hand digs in

____ Strong leg thrust while top arm pushes water

**Follow-Through
Phase**

____ Long glide; exhalation

Step 22   Kneeling Dive

CAUTION! WATER DEPTH IS CRITICAL FOR ALL DIVING SKILLS!

This step requires a minimum of 5 feet of water depth *if the deck from which you are diving is not over 1 foot higher than the water*. IF THE DECK OR PLATFORM FROM WHICH YOU ARE DIVING IS MORE THAN 1 FOOT ABOVE THE WATER, YOU MUST HAVE A WATER DEPTH OF 8 TO 10 FEET FOR SAFETY IN THIS STEP. Inadequate water depth could result in serious injury, including concussion, broken neck, quadriplegia, or death.

With adequate water depth, this kneeling dive is both safe and easy to learn. No person can claim to be a true swimmer without the ability to do a passable standing front dive with confidence.

WHY IS THE KNEELING DIVE IMPORTANT?

The kneeling dive is the first step in learning an easy standing dive. It teaches you how to enter the water smoothly, how to emerge from a dive, and how to do a shallow dive, which is one way of avoiding injury. Do not skip this important step on the way to becoming an accomplished diver.

HOW TO DO A KNEELING DIVE

If the deck height is less than 12 inches, and there is at least 5 feet of water depth, stand at the edge of the pool and hook the toes of one foot over the edge. Kneel on the opposite knee. Stretch your arms overhead, intertwine your thumbs, and squeeze your arms against your ears. It is important to keep your ears buried between your arms. Bend over until your hands are slanting down toward the water. Rock forward, take a breath and hold it, keep your chin down, and push off with your toes. Lift your rear leg. Push *out* into the water, holding your breath. Underwater, arch slightly, point your hands and head upward, and rise to the surface (see Figure 22.1).

Figure 22.1   Keys to Success: *Kneeling Dive*

Preparation Phase

1. Toes over edge, kneel on opposite knee
2. Arms over ears, squeeze
3. Lean over, point hands at water

Execution Phase

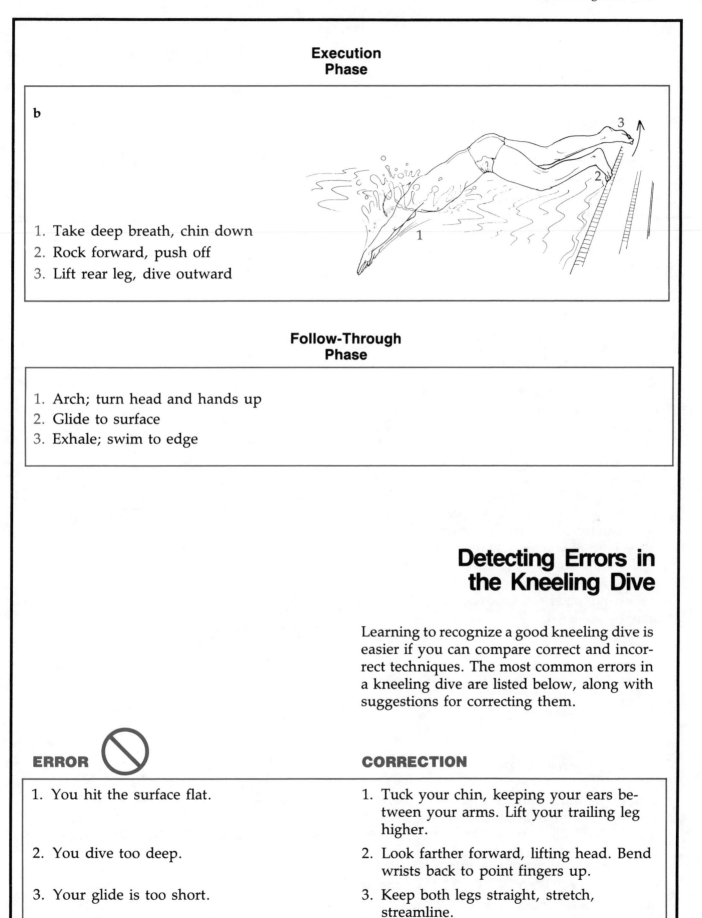

b

1. Take deep breath, chin down
2. Rock forward, push off
3. Lift rear leg, dive outward

Follow-Through Phase

1. Arch; turn head and hands up
2. Glide to surface
3. Exhale; swim to edge

Detecting Errors in the Kneeling Dive

Learning to recognize a good kneeling dive is easier if you can compare correct and incorrect techniques. The most common errors in a kneeling dive are listed below, along with suggestions for correcting them.

ERROR	CORRECTION
1. You hit the surface flat.	1. Tuck your chin, keeping your ears between your arms. Lift your trailing leg higher.
2. You dive too deep.	2. Look farther forward, lifting head. Bend wrists back to point fingers up.
3. Your glide is too short.	3. Keep both legs straight, stretch, streamline.

Kneeling Dive Drills

1. Underwater Glide

In chest-deep water, back against wall, stretch your arms overhead covering your ears. Put one foot against the wall behind you, take a breath, put your face down, aim your hands slightly downward to dig into the water, and push off. Streamline and glide underwater as far as you can.

Success Goal = 10 underwater glides

Your Score = (#) _____ underwater glides

2. Glide Through the Hoop

Get a hula hoop that floats. Tie a small weight to it, so it sinks but stands on edge on the bottom. Set it about 8 feet from the wall in 5-foot depth. Standing with your back to the wall, stretch your arms overhead, covering your ears by interlocking your thumbs and squeezing your arms tight to your ears. Take a big breath, put your face in the water, and tuck both legs. In a facedown, tucked position, place both of your feet against the wall, aim "downhill" toward the hoop, and push off underwater. Glide through the hoop and turn your hands and head up to rise (hoop distance may be adjusted).

Success Goal = 10 successful passes through the hoop

Your Score = (#) _____ passes

3. Kneeling Dive

Out of the water, move to the pool edge next to a water depth of at least 5 feet. Kneel at the edge, which should be no more than 12 inches above the water. ANY HIGHER DECK OR PLATFORM REQUIRES A MINIMUM OF 8 TO 10 FEET OF WATER DEPTH. Do a kneeling dive as described in Figure 22.1.

Success Goal = 10 kneeling dives in good form

Your Score = (#) _____ kneeling dives

4. Kneeling Dive Through the Hoop

Sink a hula hoop in 5 feet of water, about 10 to 12 feet from the edge. In deeper water, the weight holding the hoop can be tied by a line that allows the hoop to float about 5 feet beneath the surface. Two weights and two lines to the hoop will be needed to keep the hoop from turning. Do a kneeling dive and glide through the hoop before returning to the surface.

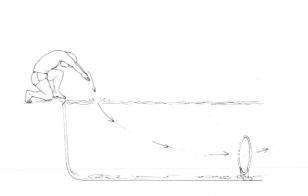

Success Goal = 5 successful dives through the hoop

Your Score = (#) _____ dives

5. Kneeling Dive With Turn Through the Hoop

Place a hula hoop on the bottom in 5 or 6 feet of water or suspend it from the bottom by two weights and two lines in deeper water. Turn the hoop so it is edge-on to you. Do a kneeling dive and make a glide with a right-angled turn to pass through the hoop.

Success Goal = 5 dives in good form (the glide and turn are incidental)

Your Score = (#) _____ dives in good form

6. Multi-Hoop Dive

In water at least 5 feet deep, place a series of weighted hoops about 3 feet apart. Do a kneeling dive and see how many hoops you can *glide* through. Swimming underwater is cheating!

Success Goal = 5 dives in good form (the long glide is incidental)

Your Score = (#) _____ dives

Kneeling Dive
Keys to Success Checklist

Success in diving is all a subjective judgment. Your glide distance or number of dives has nothing to do with success. *How* you perform the items on the checklist below, or your form while diving, determines your success. Find a qualified person to judge your technique qualitatively.

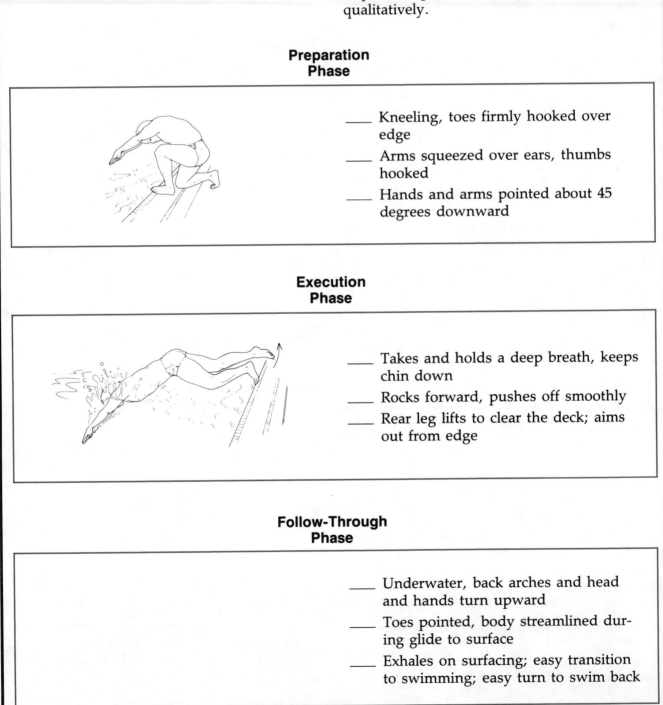

Preparation Phase

____ Kneeling, toes firmly hooked over edge

____ Arms squeezed over ears, thumbs hooked

____ Hands and arms pointed about 45 degrees downward

Execution Phase

____ Takes and holds a deep breath, keeps chin down

____ Rocks forward, pushes off smoothly

____ Rear leg lifts to clear the deck; aims out from edge

Follow-Through Phase

____ Underwater, back arches and head and hands turn upward

____ Toes pointed, body streamlined during glide to surface

____ Exhales on surfacing; easy transition to swimming; easy turn to swim back

Step 23 One-Foot Dive

CAUTION! THIS DIVE REQUIRES A WATER DEPTH OF AT LEAST 10 FEET! You have learned to do a shallow dive that carries you out at a shallow angle. Expert divers try to enter the water vertically, a stretched, vertical entry with very little splash is the mark of a good dive. Adequate water depth is required for safety because a vertical entry carries you deeper.

WHY IS A ONE-FOOT DIVE IMPORTANT?

The one-foot dive is a transition from a low-position, shallow dive to a stand-up dive that can be used from nearly any height. The one-foot dive can be learned from the deck to gain confidence, then taken to a low diving board for a new experience. It is important because it helps eliminate painful flat dives—belly flops—that result from skipping progressive steps.

HOW TO DO A ONE-FOOT DIVE

WITH A WATER DEPTH OF 10 FEET OR MORE, stand with one foot forward, one back, gripping the pool edge with the toes of your forward foot. Extend both arms overhead, covering your ears. Hook your thumbs and squeeze. Bend forward. Aim at a point only 3 feet from the edge. Point the toe of your rear foot. Lift your rear leg high over your head as you rock forward into the water. KEEP YOUR FORWARD KNEE LOCKED STRAIGHT to keep you a safe distance from the pool wall. Enter the water vertically. Keep your hands over your head for protection. When submerged, tuck your knees and turn back to the surface. Pull downward with both arms to aid in surfacing (see Figure 23.1).

Figure 23.1 Keys to Success: *One-Foot Dive*

Preparation Phase

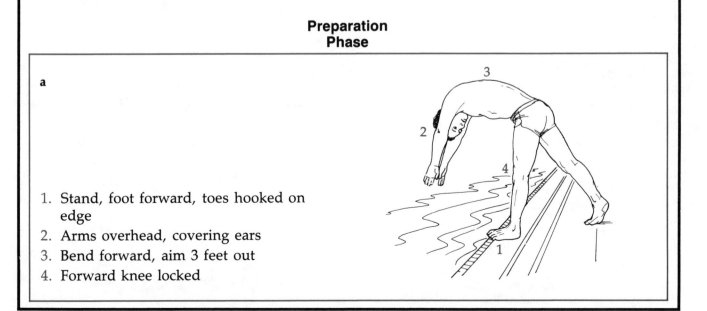

a

1. Stand, foot forward, toes hooked on edge
2. Arms overhead, covering ears
3. Bend forward, aim 3 feet out
4. Forward knee locked

Execution Phase

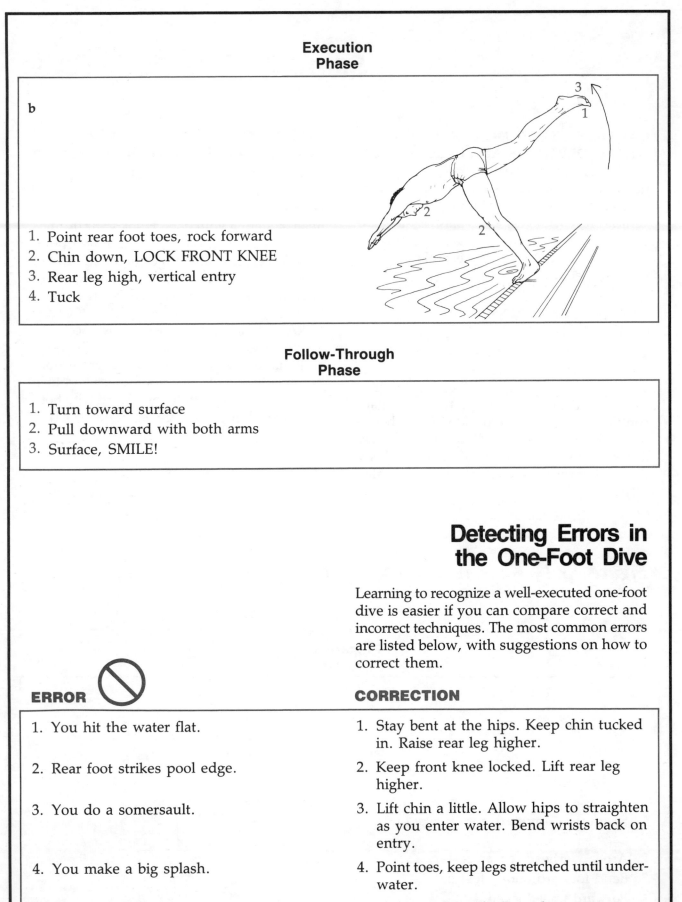

b

1. Point rear foot toes, rock forward
2. Chin down, LOCK FRONT KNEE
3. Rear leg high, vertical entry
4. Tuck

Follow-Through Phase

1. Turn toward surface
2. Pull downward with both arms
3. Surface, SMILE!

Detecting Errors in the One-Foot Dive

Learning to recognize a well-executed one-foot dive is easier if you can compare correct and incorrect techniques. The most common errors are listed below, with suggestions on how to correct them.

ERROR ⊘

CORRECTION

1. You hit the water flat.

2. Rear foot strikes pool edge.

3. You do a somersault.

4. You make a big splash.

5. You "crumble" into water.

1. Stay bent at the hips. Keep chin tucked in. Raise rear leg higher.

2. Keep front knee locked. Lift rear leg higher.

3. Lift chin a little. Allow hips to straighten as you enter water. Bend wrists back on entry.

4. Point toes, keep legs stretched until underwater.

5. Be brave, have faith, and try again.

One-Foot Dive Drills
(Water at least 10 feet deep)

1. Transition From Kneeling Dive

Do one *kneeling* dive, then prepare for a second kneeling dive. This time, before you push off, put all your weight on your forward foot and the toes of your rear foot; raise your knee about 6 inches off the deck so you are in a "track start" position. Dive. (Do not use a hoop.)

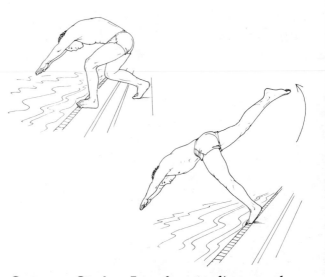

Success Goal = 5 track start dives, each one a little higher than the last

Your Score = (#) _____ track start dives

2. Correct One-Foot Dive

Start as in Drill 1 but straighten your forward knee and lock it straight. Aim closer in to the side and do a one-foot dive as in Figure 23.1.

Success Goal = 10 one-foot dives with vertical entry, straight legs, pointed toes, and no splash

Your Score = (#) _____ one-foot dives

3. Low Board Dive

Hook the toes of one foot over the end of the 1-meter diving board. Do not bounce the board. Lift your chin so you are looking out just over your fingertips, aiming at a point about 4 feet out. Keep your forward knee rigid, but lift your rear leg a little less vigorously. Do a one-foot dive.

Success Goal = 5 one-foot dives in good form from the 1-meter board

Your Score = (#) _____ one-foot dives

One-Foot Dive Keys to Success Checklist

Qualitative assessment of diving skills is necessary to evaluate technique. You have been meeting quantitative goals as a means of practice, but now it is time for someone to make a qualitative evaluation. Ask a knowledgeable person to use the checklist below for this purpose.

Preparation Phase

_____ Stands with one foot forward, toes firmly hooked over pool edge

_____ Arms overhead covering ears, thumbs hooked

_____ Bends forward at waist, hands aimed at water 3 feet out from edge

_____ Forward knee locked in straight position

Execution Phase

___ Points toes on rear foot, rocks forward to put weight on forward foot

___ Chin down, FRONT KNEE LOCKED for safety

___ Tips forward, lifts rear leg high over head and makes a vertical entry

___ Underwater, tucks knees to slow descent

Follow-Through Phase

___ Turns toward surface

___ Ascends by pulling downward with both arms

___ Surfaces SMILING

Step 24 Standing Forward Dive

CAUTION! LEARN THIS STEP IN A MINIMUM WATER DEPTH OF 10 FEET!

A standing front dive is one of the basic skills of personal proficiency. It is used as a means for entering the water, but it also is a telltale mark of an accomplished swimmer. It allows the swimmer to enter the water with grace and precision; it is as much aesthetic as utilitarian.

WHY IS A STANDING FRONT DIVE IMPORTANT?

Diving is a sport separate from, but closely related to, swimming. The standing front dive is the primary, elementary technique in a whole series of more complex skills. It is not important to swimming per se but is a skill expected of, and desired by, nearly all swimmers. It is important in that it may open an entirely new area of sport interest for you. Try it—you'll like it.

HOW TO DO A STANDING FRONT DIVE

Be sure you have at least 10 feet of water depth and no underwater obstructions. Stand with the toes of both feet gripping the pool edge, your arms at your side. Swing both arms in a small circle (a foot in diameter)—out, back, around, and forward—past your hips. As your arms circle, bend your knees slightly. As your arms pass your hips, spring upward. Bend fully at your waist, lifting your hips behind you. Continue the arm swing until your hands point 4 feet out from the edge. Tuck your head between your arms and lift both legs behind you, straight and stretched. Enter the water vertically. Tuck your knees, or arch and turn your head and arms upward, to glide to the surface (see Figure 24.1).

Figure 24.1 Keys to Success: *Standing Forward Dive*

**Preparation
Phase**

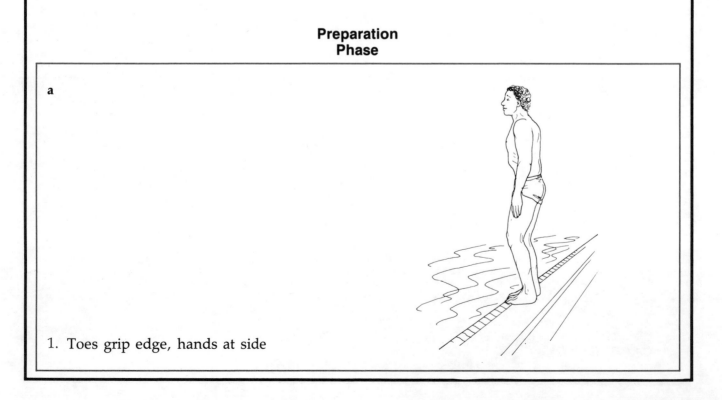

a

1. Toes grip edge, hands at side

Execution
Phase

b

1. Circle arms, bend knees

c

2. Spring upward, lift hips

d

3. Point 4 feet out, bend double

e

4. Tuck chin, lift legs

f

5. Body straight, vertical entry

Follow-Through
Phase

1. Tuck knees or arch; lift head, arms
2. Rise or glide to surface

Detecting Errors in the Standing Front Dive

Learning to recognize a well-executed standing front dive is easier if you can compare correct and incorrect techniques. The most common errors in the standing front dive are listed below, along with suggestions on how to correct them.

ERROR 🚫

CORRECTION

1. You hit the water flat.

2. You dive too far out.

3. Legs are apart.

4. Knees are bent.

5. Toes are not pointed.

1. Think somersault; a dive is one half of a somersault. Tuck chin, get hips up behind you, lift legs, get more spring.

2. Jump up, not out. Imagine diving over a low fence 1 foot in front of you and landing just on the other side. Think about jumping into a handstand on the water 3 feet out. Aim for the bottom.

3. Squeeze!

4. Stretch!

5. Whose toes are they?

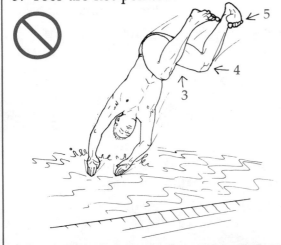

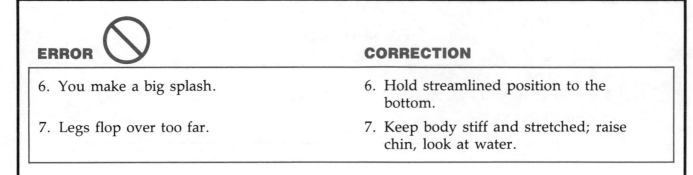

ERROR 🚫	**CORRECTION**
6. You make a big splash.	6. Hold streamlined position to the bottom.
7. Legs flop over too far.	7. Keep body stiff and stretched; raise chin, look at water.

Standing Front Dive Drills

1. Standing, Two-Footed Fall-In Dive

This drill may be performed from any low elevation, but it works best from about 12 inches above water level. With water 10 feet or more in depth, stand with both feet at the edge of the pool. Grip the edge firmly with the toes of both feet. Extend both arms overhead, covering your ears. Hook your thumbs together. Squeeze your arms against your ears. Bend over until your hands point to the water about 3 feet from the edge. Do not allow your knees to bend at any time during the dive. Bend·your wrists back slightly. Dive. When submerged, lift your chin, turn your arms and hands upward, arch your back, and glide outward and upward. Pull toward the top if you wish to hurry the ascent.

Success Goal = 3 fall-in dives, or until the dive is comfortable

Your Score = (#) _____ fall-in dives

2. Hands-Down, Fall-In Dive

Start as above but leave your hands at your sides. As you bend over and start your fall, bring your hands forward into the dive position.

Success Goal = 3 hands-down dives, or until comfortable

Your Score = (#) _____ hands-down dives

3. Fall-In Dive With Spring

Start as in Drill 2 but bend your knees slightly before starting to fall. Keep them bent until you are falling and are *definitely off-balance*, then jump with your legs and lift them behind you. You will straighten your legs in the process of jumping; keep them straight for the entry.

Success Goal = 3 fall-and-spring dives

Your Score = (#) _____ fall-and-spring dives

4. Arm-Swing Dive With Spring

Stand erect at the edge of the pool, toes gripping the edge. Do *not* dive, but practice swinging your arms in a small circle forward past your legs a few times. Swing your arms out, around, and forward in a one-foot circle. Each time they come forward, bend and straighten your knees slightly as if you were preparing to jump. After several practice swings, think about your fall-and-spring dives and imagine bending over *as* you swing your arms forward and springing directly into a handstand on top of the water. DO IT!

Success Goal = 5 arm-swing spring dives

Your Score = (#) _____ arm-swing spring dives

5. Fully Coordinated Standing Front Dive

Do a standing forward dive as described in Figure 24.1.

Success Goal = 10 standing front dives

Your Score = (#) _____ standing front dives

6. Hula Hoop-for-Height Dive

Stand within a hula hoop ready for a standing front dive. Have someone hold the hoop at about shin or knee height, so that the hoop is about a foot in front of your legs. (Have him or her hold it from the side, so you won't kick them with your heels.) Dive up and over the hoop, being careful to get your head down for a *vertical* entry. Keep your entries close to the wall (within 4 feet). Raise the hoop a little at a time to see how high you can dive to clear it.

Success Goal = 10 standing hoop dives at knee height

Your Score = (#) _____ standing hoop dives at knee height

7. Dive Through the Ring

DO NOT USE A HULA HOOP FOR THIS DIVE: IT HURTS! Get a piece of floating line (such as polypropylene) and tie a ring about 4 feet in diameter. Float it on the water at varying distances from the edge, but no closer than 2 feet. Try to do a good standing front dive through the ring. Dive quickly, because it floats into all sorts of nonring shapes if you wait too long. Keep your entries vertical.

Success Goal = 5 *good form* dives through the ring (they don't count if they are sloppy)

Your Score = (#) _____ *good form* dives

8. Fully Coordinated Standing Front Dive From Low Board

Stand on the end of the 1-meter diving board, toes over the edge. Notice that as you practice arm circles, the board bounces. Get your arm circles in rhythm with the board's bounce, count the arm circles, and use the upward movement of the board to give you more height on your dive. Keep your chin up more; the board will lift your legs.

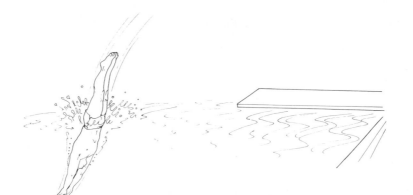

Success Goal = 10 successful board dives with a streamlined, vertical entry

Your Score = (#) _____ board dives

Standing Front Dive
Keys to Success Checklist

Reflexes and your kinesthetic sense of movement, which tells you the position of your body in the air, are important to your development as a diver. It is difficult to measure these by yourself. Ask a trained observer to evaluate your skill with the use of this checklist.

Preparation Phase

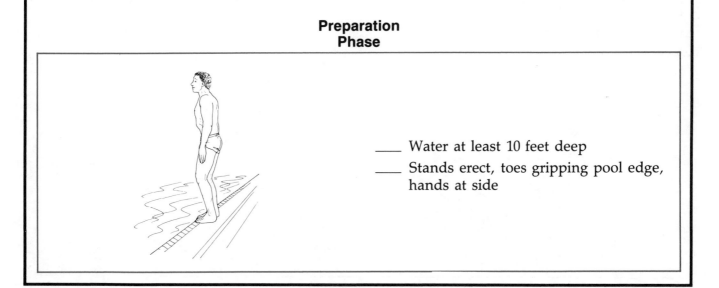

_____ Water at least 10 feet deep

_____ Stands erect, toes gripping pool edge, hands at side

Execution
Phase

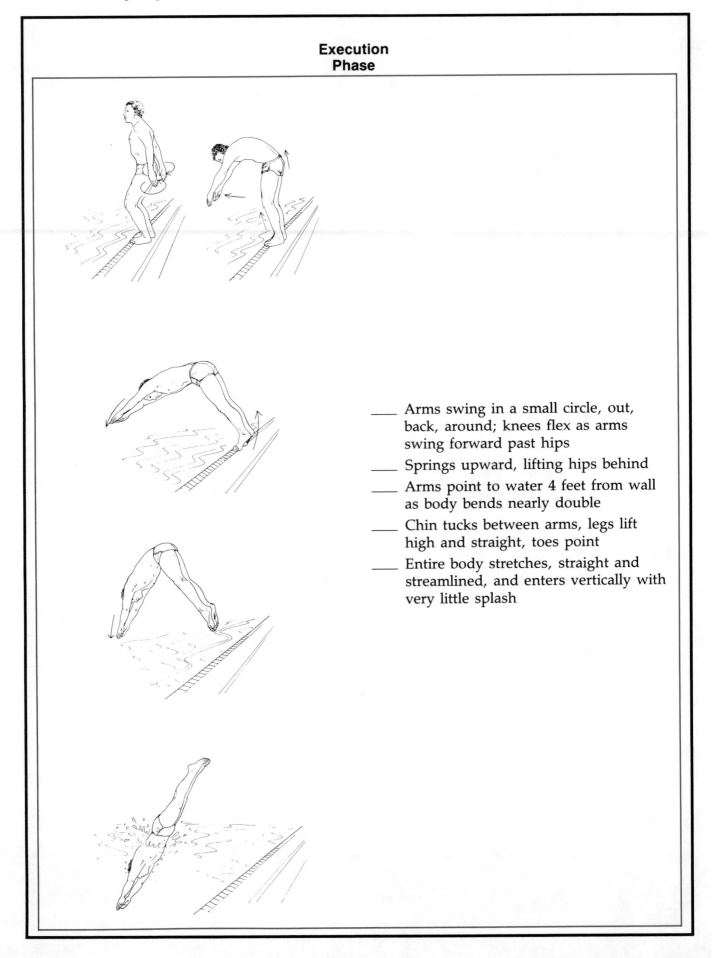

_____ Arms swing in a small circle, out, back, around; knees flex as arms swing forward past hips

_____ Springs upward, lifting hips behind

_____ Arms point to water 4 feet from wall as body bends nearly double

_____ Chin tucks between arms, legs lift high and straight, toes point

_____ Entire body stretches, straight and streamlined, and enters vertically with very little splash

Follow-Through
Phase

_____ Tucks knees to slow descent; or arches back, lifts head and hands for glide

_____ Rises or glides to surface

Rating Your Total Progress

There have been several Success Goals within this swimming course. However, you have been working on both physical and psychological skills. The following self-rating inventory should lead you to some interesting conclusions. Read the questions thoughtfully and answer them with care.

PSYCHOLOGICAL SKILLS

Perhaps the very greatest success you can imagine is the change in the way you feel about the water. This psychological achievement is probably the most important.

To what degree have you overcome your fear of water?

_____ Complete

_____ Some

_____ Zero

_____ Still maintain a healthy respect

What is your ability to save yourself if you were to fall into the water unexpectedly?

_____ Great

_____ Don't know

_____ Zero

Have you improved significantly in confidence?

_____ Yes

_____ No

Do you enjoy the water?

_____ Much

_____ Quite a bit

_____ Some

_____ Not at all

Did you have fun in class?

_____ Lots

_____ Some

_____ None

PHYSICAL SKILLS

The second general success goal in a swimming course is the physical progress you have made. How do you rate yourself on the strokes and dives that you learned?

	Very Good	Good	Okay	Poor
Back float	_____	_____	_____	_____
Sculling	_____	_____	_____	_____
Back support kick	_____	_____	_____	_____
Back propulsion kick	_____	_____	_____	_____
Elementary backstroke arm motion	_____	_____	_____	_____
Prone beginner stroke	_____	_____	_____	_____
Turning over	_____	_____	_____	_____
Crawl stroke	_____	_____	_____	_____
Breaststroke kick	_____	_____	_____	_____
Whole breaststroke	_____	_____	_____	_____
Coordinated elementary backstroke	_____	_____	_____	_____
Scissors kick	_____	_____	_____	_____
Coordinated sidestroke	_____	_____	_____	_____
Standing front dive	_____	_____	_____	_____

OVERALL SWIMMING PROGRESS

Considering all the psychological and physical factors you marked above, how would you rate yourself in this course? Are you pleased with your progress?

_____ Very successful

_____ Successful

_____ Fairly successful

_____ Barely successful

_____ Unsuccessful

ADDITIONAL COMMENTS AND QUESTIONS

Add any questions you believe should have been asked—and answer them too. Then, reflect a bit on the profile that emerges. What were your strong points? Your weak points? Where are you going from here? Do you care enough to put more time and effort into strengthening those weak points? What was lacking or superfluous in the course? Were weaknesses due to the course or to the instructor?

Appendix

Individual Program

INDIVIDUAL COURSE IN _____ GRADE/COURSE SECTION _____

STUDENT'S NAME _____ STUDENT ID # _____

SKILLS/CONCEPTS	TECHNIQUE AND PERFORMANCE OBJECTIVES	WT* ×	POINT PROGRESS** =				FINAL SCORE***
			1	2	3	4	

Note. From ''The Role of Expert Knowledge Structures in an Instructional Design Model for Physical Education'' by J.N. Vickers, 1983, *Journal of Teaching in Physical Education,* **2**(3), p. 17. Copyright 1983 by Joan N. Vickers. Adapted by permission.

*WT = Weighting of an objective's degree of difficulty.

**PROGRESS = Ongoing success, which may be expressed in terms of (a) accumulated points (1, 2, 3, 4); (b) grades (D, C, B, A); (c) symbols (merit, bronze, silver, gold); (d) unsatisfactory/satisfactory; and others as desired.

***FINAL SCORE equals WT times PROGRESS.

About the Author

David G. Thomas has been a swimming teacher and coach since 1948, when he became a water safety field representative for the American National Red Cross. In 1955 he became swimming coach and director of aquatics at Berea High School, Berea, Ohio. Eight years later he moved to the State University of New York at Binghamton, where he was director of aquatics and swimming coach until retiring as professor emeritus in 1985.

Thomas gained nationwide prominence in 1972 by producing a textbook, a teaching guide, exams, and visual aids for training swimming pool operators. The *Swimming Pool Operators Handbook* and the other materials were published by the National Swimming Pool Foundation as the basis for their Certified Pool Operators program.

Thomas has published many articles on aquatic subjects and is a contributing author to several books on swimming pool design and operation. He has been writing extensively since retirement, with his most recent book being *Competitive Swimming Management* (Leisure Press, 1988). Soon to be released is *Professional Aquatic Management*, co-authored with Robert Clayton (Leisure Press, 1989). Self-employed as a consultant in aquatics and pool design and operation, Thomas lives with his wife, Virginia, in Anderson, SC. He enjoys scuba diving and boating in his leisure time and swims a mile or more each day for fitness.